A View from the Hill

A View from the Hill

A History of Humboldt State University

by William R. Tanner, PhD

published by University Graphic Services,
Humboldt State University, Arcata, California
1993

Table of Contents

This history of Humboldt State
University is dedicated to the memory of
"Mr. Humboldt," Homer P. Balabanis (1897-1991).
From 1923 until his death,
he served this university as faculty
member, administrator, and booster of
"the Humboldt Spirit."

Foreword

This volume is not meant to be a comprehensive institutional history. Rather, it is an attempt to record a social memory for former students, faculty, staff, and administrators. Thus the reader will discover an emphasis on the *people* of Humboldt State.

The creation of this volume was a collective effort. Associations and conversations with Homer P. Balabanis inspired the book. President Alistair McCrone encouraged it. A university sabbatical leave of one semester provided the necessary time for most of the research.

Many people provided information and some provided photographs, including Gladys Burritt, Connie Carlson, Jean Falor, James Gast, Mary Greta, Paul Hendrickson, Vern Henricks, Gayle Karshner, June McCartney, Dan Pambianco, Dana Rice, Virginia Rumble, Howard Seemann, Mr. and Mrs. Henry Sorenson, Helen Stover, Bill Sullivan, Tom Trepiak, and Edward Webb. Several students helped with research and conducted oral interviews. Among them were Jeanie Allard, Edie Butler, Joe Coohill, Clark Hatch, and Chris Hopkins. At various stages, portions of the manuscript were typed by Linda Hall-Martin, Judy Kirsch, Kathy Mayer, and Delores McBroome.

Those who read parts or all of the manuscript, correcting errors and making suggestions, were Milton Dobkin, Patsy Givins, John Hennessy, Gayle Karshner, Alistair McCrone, and Rod Sievers. Many thanks to all of these, as well as to Erich Schimps, Lincoln Kilian, and other personnel in the Humboldt Room of the university library.

Thanks to Simpson Paper Company for their donation of the cover stock and part of the text paper. Thanks also to Brizard Company, Simpson Timber Company and Arcata Redwood Company for their financial support in the production of this book.

Finally, most credit for the making of this book goes to Kathleen Heil and her staff in University Graphic Services. She and Dar Spain, with assistance from Erich Schimps, selected photographs and created an attractive design for this volume. Jim Toms assisted Dar Spain in making prints of all the photos. Tim Sims, assisted by Julie Steiner, edited and rearranged parts of the manuscript and wrote some of the special features for publication.

Without all these people, we would not have a published history of this institution.

The reader may find mistakes or may be disappointed by the omission of a name, a story, or an event associated with his or her own experiences at Humboldt State. For that, we apologize. Those names, stories, and events mentioned in this little volume are meant only to be representative of the larger experience of Humboldt since 1913. Future revisions of this history can correct any omissions.

William R. Tanner
Professor of History

The effort to establish Humboldt Normal School was fraught with uncertainty and controversy. Three hundred miles from San Francisco, this area was mainly rural during the first decade of the 20th century. The founding of a college on this isolated coast presented a number of challenges: limited transportation, lack of facilities, few faculty available, and distance from the seat of state government, to name but a few.

The normal first opened its doors in the spring of 1914, in facilities leased from the Arcata Grammar School. Probably no one of that era envisioned a thriving university such as would exist eight decades later. In those early years, survival was enough of a concern.

A national wave of social progressivism (p 2) had prepared the way. Education had become a national priority around the turn of the century, accenting the need for more, and better trained, schoolteachers. Locally, Humboldt's normal school (a *normal* trained elementary teachers, primarily) owed its existence to months of arduous preparation. Political maneuvering dominated the effort: in particular, a contest between the cities of Eureka and Arcata over the school's location.

The Politics of a New School

Eureka's chamber of commerce apparently made the first move toward establishing a normal school in Humboldt County. In late 1911, Eureka appointed a committee comprised of George Burchard, Charles Stern, and E.A. Leach, to mount public support and make overtures to Sacramento. Burchard later moved to Arcata and headed a chamber of commerce effort to locate the normal school there. Stern was later appointed by Governor Johnson to the newly created state board of education, where he served as an important spokesperson for the North Coast.

The committee brought forward many arguments to sway legislators. Foremost were the area's isolation and the long distance from a teacher-training institution (Southern Oregon Normal in Ashland was closest — 200 miles away).

Most passenger traffic in and out of Humboldt County came by water. The Northwest Pacific Railroad was coming from the south, but not until 1914 would Fort Seward residents witness the driving of the final spike in the line connecting Sausalito and Eureka. The Arcata & Mad River Railroad could bring students from Korbel and Blue Lake. From Crescent City, however, they had to wait up to six hours for high tide to make the Klamath River navigable by ferry, then progress slowly southward by car or (more likely) horse-drawn wagon. Prior to 1914, only one poor dirt road, the Humboldt and Mendocino Wagon Road, served these travelers. Roads to Redding stood unimproved.

Sixty-five percent of the teachers in the area were not certified. Without a North Coast normal school, they, and any future teachers, would have to bear the expense of attending school in Oregon or San Francisco. Humboldt County also shared in the statewide shortage of qualified teachers due to increased public school attendance. A 1911 state assembly decision to distribute funds according to average daily attendance had had the effect of a compulsory school attendance law.

The Eureka normal committee mounted these and other arguments. With some reluctance, they left out of their proposals the controversial matter of a site for the normal school in order to enlist support from other communities. A new agency, the Federated Commercial Bodies of Humboldt County, headed by Eurekan William Cook, joined the committee in seeking countywide support.

In December, 1912, State Senator William Kehoe and Assemblyman Hans Nelson introduced legislation to establish a Humboldt County normal school. Rumor has it that the governor was unenthusiastic, but a local Republi-

Progressive Education

researched by the author

The founding of Humboldt State coincided with an exciting era of reform, the Progressive Movement (roughly 1897-1917), which brought education to new prominence on the national agenda. The Progressives sought to alleviate the negative consequences of industrialism. They wanted a nation economically equitable and socially just with increased political participation by the masses. For all of this, education was key. Historian Lawrence Cremin defined progressive education as

part of a vast humanitarian effort to apply the promise of American life — the ideal of government by, of, and for the people — to the puzzling new urban industrial civilization . . . a many-sided effort to use schools to improve the lives of individuals.

The reforms that began in the cities in the 1890s, soon spread to state politics and eventually found leadership in the administrations of two presidents, Theodore Roosevelt and Woodrow Wilson. Reformers regulated public utilities and big business, created safety and sanitation laws, fought state and city political bosses, and pushed through legislation on women's suffrage, prohibition, and compulsory school attendance.

California experienced this reform under the principal leadership of Governor Hiram Johnson (later U.S. senator and sidekick to President Teddy Roosevelt). For a quarter century prior to Johnson's governorship,

California had lived under the thumb of the powerful Southern Pacific Railroad, which controlled the workings of government so as to keep competitive railroads and shipping lines from moving into the state. But when progressive Republicans (those breaking from GOP ranks), and Democrats sent Hiram Johnson and other reformers to Sacramento, the assembly put into effect many of the aforementioned reforms (including regulation of the railroads).

The reform atmosphere created a more receptive environment for proposals to establish new normal schools. (Fresno State Normal was established in 1911; Humboldt State Normal in 1913.)

can politico and friend of the governor, Ralph Waldo Bull, lobbied vigorously for passage. Governor Johnson signed the law on June 16, 1913, establishing "Humboldt State Normal School, for the training and education of teachers and others in the art of instructing and governing the public schools of this state."

Johnson also appointed a local board of trustees and empowered them to hire and fire employees, and to establish admission and curriculum standards. The board reported once a year to the state superintendent of instruction. Local members included William Cook, Henry Bridges, and Charlotte Gale, all of Eureka; Rease Wiley of Arcata; and Edward Haight of Fortuna. The governor and state superintendent served as *ex officio* members.

The Feud: Eureka vs. Arcata

Thus was achieved stage one of the ultimate goal. The second stage, however, would prove more difficult: choosing a location for the school.

Eureka, the county seat, seemed the logical place. It was centrally located and had the largest population in the county (11,845). It could offer more facilities for the school and for student housing. Furthermore, the Northwestern Pacific Railroad would soon reach Eureka, providing transportation by land from the south. Since three of five board members lived in Eureka, few doubted the location would be there. But while Eurekans *assumed* they would get the normal school, Arcatans were not conceding anything.

Legislation establishing the normal school authorized the local board to select a site and provide buildings. The state assembly had appropriated $10,000 to fund the school,

Joy Gastman Sr.'s 1913 cartoon about the disagreement over the location of the Normal School. Charlotte Gale is shown escaping around the corner of city hall.

provided they could obtain a two-year lease, free of charge, for a suitable building. The board met on November 6, 1913, and determined that the school would open the following January. Board secretary Charlotte Gale sent letters to the Arcata, Eureka, and Fortuna chambers of commerce notifying them of a November 13 meeting accepting proposals for the location of the school. The letter read, in part:

> Those wishing to secure the location must, according to the law, bring a two-year lease of suitable rooms or building, free of charge, for the housing of said school.

The Arcata Chamber of Commerce, led by J.F. Benton, William Preston, W.W. Stone, J.J. Krohn, Henry Brizard, and former Eurekan George Burchard, produced a convincing written proposal. They garnered pledges totaling $12,000 from residents in Arcata and as far north as Trinidad. They also acquired a two-year lease on the Arcata Grammar School, the cooperation and use of faculty and facilities at Arcata High School, use of twenty acres of land for agricultural experiments, rooms in local residences to house as many as 100 students, and a twelve-and-a-half acre site belonging to William Preston.

They presented this offer to the trustees on November 13. The Eureka and Fortuna proposals, presented orally, were not as appealing nor as firm. Fortuna offered twenty acres of land and use of a five-room building. Eureka offered use of the Winship building the following July and an indefinite sum of money.

To the consternation of her fellow Eurekans, trustee Charlotte Gale joined Rease Wiley of Arcata and Edward Haight of Fortuna in accepting the Arcata proposal (a 3-2 vote).

3

They set January 5, 1914, as the opening day and appointed Nelson Blieau Van Matré, then superintendent of Eureka public schools, as president of the normal school.

William Cook and the Eurekans fought back. They challenged the legality of the board's decision on the basis that two board members had not been invited, namely, Governor Johnson and Superintendent Edward Hyatt. (Both were in Sacramento and probably unaware of the meeting.) An appeal to the state attorney general resulted in the November 13 meeting being declared invalid, thus negating the decision in favor of Arcata.

After informing the governor and superintendent, three other meetings were scheduled for late November and early December. Eurekans busily drew up a more formal written proposal to present at these meetings. The governor and superintendent still could not attend. Arcata supporters Wiley and Haight boycotted the meetings on the presumption that Charlotte Gale would now join her Eurekan colleagues in reversing the earlier decision.

A period of bitterness between the two communities ensued. (These communities had been feuding since 1854 over the series of disputed elections that determined the Humboldt County seat.) Editorial battles raged between the *Humboldt Standard* and the *Arcata Union*. The former argued Eureka was the logical place for the normal school. The latter maintained Arcata had made a legitimate offer which had been accepted and should not be rescinded.

As the bickering went on, Wiley and Haight arranged a February 4 board meeting in Sacramento with Superintendent Hyatt and Governor Johnson attending. At that meeting, Cook and Bridges voted again to rescind the Arcata location. Charlotte Gale, who had indeed felt the wrath of many Eurekans, now switched her vote. The board as a whole, however, voted 4-3 to reaffirm the November 13 decision in favor of Arcata.

Perhaps Arcata had more than just its offer to recommend it. Former HSU faculty members Homer Balabanis and Hyman Palais conjectured that Arcata's political clout in Sacramento influenced the decision. Arcatan Ralph Bull, for

instance, was a friend of Governor Johnson. Alexander Brizard, father of Arcatan Henry Brizard, was a close associate of Arcata native, P.E. Bowles, a University of California regent in Oakland whose daughter married the governor's son. So it's possible that Governor Johnson could have been swayed by the Arcata connections.

Reconciliation

Shortly after that February meeting, in reply to a *Union* editorial asking Eureka and Arcata to "bury the hatchet," the *Humboldt Standard* affirmed:

> The *Standard* is pleased to say to the *Union* and Arcatans generally that there is no hatchet to bury. Eureka wants the Normal School to be a success . . . Forget the contest and go to work making the institution a power. Eureka is with you.

Go to work they did. It had taken nearly eight months to decide where to locate the school. It would take only two months to make it operable.

In early March, Van Matré assumed the presidency and presented the trustees with acceptable standards for a course of study. Shortly thereafter, the board issued the first bulletin for use by prospective students. The board also made plans for the state's $10,000 and called in the $12,000 in pledges made earlier.

That first budget for Humboldt State Normal School was $17,248. Salaries commanded $10,000, and $3,291 went toward constructing an additional building on the grounds of the grammar school, located on 11th and M Streets (now the site of Copeland Lumber). The remainder went toward library books, equipment, and labor.

The railroads cooperated by arranging schedules so commuters from the Eel River valley (as far away as Scotia) could make classes and be home for supper.

Humboldt State was to be operable April 6, 1914.

(clockwise from top) Arcata Plaza, c. 1905-15; H Street in Arcata with Methodist Church in foreground; Excelsior Logging Company train; view east on 11th Street.

Transportation and Isolation

sources:
The Humboldt Bay Region, 1850-1875, by Owen C. Coy; "California Redwood Empire Place Names," by Lynwood Carranco and Andrew Genzoli; *The Redwood Country,* edited by Lynwood Carranco

In 1850, Union (later Arcata) was the major jump-off point for the trails to the gold mines. By 1856 a major trail crossed Bald Mountain to Orleans and the Hoopa Valley, and wagon roads reached as far inland as Weaverville.

Not until 1867 would a daily stage connect Arcata and Eureka. Water travel was quicker. In 1869, a poorly maintained Mattole Road connected Petrolia and Eureka. A new road in 1875 connected Humboldt Bay with Mendocino.

Meanwhile, in 1855 Union had opened a narrow-gauge railroad on a long wooden trestle. It crossed the muddy shallows separating the town from navigable waters. This was the first operating railroad in California. Freight and passengers rode four-wheel carts pulled by draft horses. The wharf, the longest in the country, ran from the site of today's Arcata Post Office to a point two miles out into the bay.

This Arcata & Mad River Railroad soon expanded to carry the burgeoning timber industry's redwood in from the hills. The *Black Diamond* became the line's first steam locomotive in 1875.

Like Humboldt County's limited road system, the rails went into and out of the mountains, but no line actually went out of the area. Most goods and passengers came and went by ship. Sea passage was slow, occasionally dangerous, and impossible to schedule with any accuracy. Finally in 1914 the combined efforts of the Santa Fe and Southern Pacific produced a railroad line from Sausalito to Eureka. The Northwestern Pacific Railroad would be the last major rail line built in the country.

View north across Humboldt Bay to the Arcata Wharf.

(clockwise from top right) Steamship *Pomona* on Humboldt Bay; passenger train alongside the Arcata & Mad River Railroad Depot (now the Arcata Post Office site); ferry crossing the Klamath River; road north from Arcata to Trinidad.

7

Alexander
von Humboldt

The name of the German baron, Alexander von Humboldt (1769-1859), is affixed to a university in Berlin, mountains on four continents, a glacier in Greenland, a river in Nevada, bays in California and Colombia, a South Pacific current, and a "sea" on the dark side of the moon. Many have been the scientists and explorers to fall under the spell of the great man's intellect, including members of the 1850 *Laura Virginia* expedition who paid their tribute in the naming of Humboldt Bay.

"I have an extravagant idea," Humboldt once wrote, "of describing in one and the same work the whole material world — all that we know today of celestial bodies and of life upon the earth —from the nebular stars to the mosses on the granite rocks." Thus he began his final work, the voluminous *Kosmos.*

It was precisely that driving curiosity, that desire to observe and catalog *everything,* that led Humboldt to transform Old World perceptions and become one of the most celebrated scientists of his day. Darwin called him "the greatest scientific traveler that ever lived."

His New World expedition included a trek through Venezuelan jungles and mountains — an experience that would shed light on his world's concepts of geology, geography, biology, and ecology. He also documented the oppressive treatment of Indian slaves under Spanish rule, which led Simon Bolivar to call him "the discoverer of the New World [whose studies] have done more good than all the Conquistadors put together."

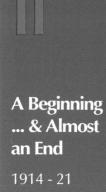

A Beginning ... & Almost an End

1914 - 21

President Van Matré

Nelson Blieau Van Matré (1873-1956), became the first president of Humboldt State Normal School in March, 1914. Van Matré had attended Dixon College, Northern Illinois College of Law, and the University of Chicago, where he earned a doctorate in education. (Chicago, a center for progressive education, had pioneered the laboratory school for teacher training in the 1890s.) Van Matré supervised and taught in elementary and secondary schools in the Midwest and California for some 15 years, then superintended Eureka city schools for a year, before becoming president of HSNS. He and his wife moved to Arcata to a home still standing on the corner of 10th and I streets. He busied himself immediately with establishing curriculum, recruiting students, and choosing faculty for the opening of school in April.

Small Beginnings

Van Matré worked with a $17,000 budget that first year. (By comparison, the 1992-93 HSU budget exceeded $52 million.) The normal's main building, Arcata Grammar School, along the railroad tracks at 11th and M streets, was "a rather drab and austere two-story frame edifice," in the words of historian Hyman Palais. Besides offices, it housed a gymnasium, manual training room, domestic science room, and library. HSNS soon added a temporary building for assemblies.

Student housing in small-town Arcata presented a challenge. Brousse Brizard's Normal Home-Finding Committee found local homes where students could purchase room and board.

Despite all obstacles, 62 students showed up for the open-

President Van Matré

ing day of school. By early May the school had 63 women and 15 men. (All forty-eight states would have compulsory education statutes by 1918, so already there was a growing need for school teachers.)

Sarah Davies, author of an early history of Humboldt State, characterized the admission requirements as judgmental. Students had to be at least 16 years of age, "reasonably mature, [having] good health, and a good moral character." They were, after all, training to become teachers of young children.

They chose from four programs:

1) a one-year course for experienced teachers,

2) a two-year course for high school graduates,

3) a three-year course for students with two or three years of high school, or

4) a four-year course for grammar school graduates.

By mid-April HSNS operated a grammar school for five grades. Under the supervision of Elizabeth Rogers, who had performed similar duties in Chico and San Diego, HSNS students taught reading, math, grammar, history, and geography to elementary school children.

Three other faculty members joined Rogers for the first session: A.J. Davis, who had been president of two normal schools in the East; Walter Clayton, a former school district superintendent from Nevada; and Emma Woodman, teacher of manual training, domestic science, and art. Salaries were $1,800 for men and $1,200 for women. President Van Matré's annual salary was $3,200.

Progressive Education

Progressive education reforms (p 2) heavily influenced the philosophy and curriculum of Humboldt State Normal School in its infancy. The nation's transition from an essentially rural agrarian state to urban industrialism had set education and political reformers to thinking about the inadequacies of the nation's schools. From centers such as Columbia University in New York, the University of Chicago, and Stanford University came the thinking that public schools should assume the instructional role once filled by agrarian living.

Thus vocational training rather than classical studies received increasing emphasis. Manual training and domestic science, with a community orientation, formed the core of school curricula nationwide. An official report of the National Education Association listed seven objectives of secondary education:

> the promotion of health, command of fundamental processes, worthy home membership, vocation, citizenship, worthy use of leisure, and ethical character.

In effect, public schools took on the socialization and moral training of youth on behalf of society at large.

The curriculum and philosophy of Humboldt State Normal would vary little from these trends. HSNS was only one of many normal schools established to train rural elementary school teachers.

Humboldt's faculty offered the following courses:

> agriculture; American literature; arithmetic methods; bookkeeping methods; domestic science; drawing; general science; geography methods; history methods; history of education; manual training; music pedagogy; penmanship and spelling methods; physical culture; psychology; reading and composition methods; teaching.

With such a comprehensive curriculum, the 1915 catalog could claim that HSNS had everything an up-to-date normal school needed to train first-rate teachers.

By 1919 vocational training (in agriculture, horticulture, domestic science, manual training, and music) was required of all students. Those courses were considered both utilitarian and educational. Katherine Asher was brought in from Arcata High School to teach another utilitarian course, physical education.

Student Life

For the HSNS student in those early days, room and board ran $20-27 per month. Two years' books cost $20-25.

Campus life involved far more than books and lectures, however. Students quickly established extracurricular activities. For instance, the 1915 catalog said HSNS would encourage "clean, wholesome athletics among both the young men and young women." Gym classes included dancing, gymnastics, calisthenics, and various playground games geared toward elementary school teachers of physical education and health education.

Many of the men engaged in long distance running — several miles out Alliance Road and back — which may have had a hand in Humboldt's strong cross-country running tradition.

Students also competed in intramural basketball, baseball, and track. The 1915 physical education class divided into two teams and ran races on the gravel in front of the school. The domestic science class served a meal to the winners. Women dominated these sports, especially after America entered the war in April, 1917.

Humboldt played its first football game, of sorts, against Fortuna High School, and lost by an overwhelming margin. Former coach Joseph Forbes, in his history of Humboldt athletics, noted that "all male students were shanghaied" to provide enough members for the football team.

To effectively train teachers so that the results of the training can be measured in terms of efficiency in school work, it is necessary to place particular emphasis upon four phases of the training.

1. A careful content review of all the subjects taught in the Elementary Schools.

2. Thorough and adaptable courses in Educational Psychology, Pedagogy, Methods of Teaching, and School Management.

3. Complete and comprehensive vocational courses. They should be given in such a manner that the information and knowledge gained can be applied directly by the teacher for the betterment, contentment, and upbuilding of the community in which she resides.

4. A very careful and systematic study of the workings of a school system. This, together with constant observation and the greatest possible amount of successful practice teaching in a well-organized training school, constitutes an important part of the course.

If you are interested in becoming a well-prepared, thorough, and efficient teacher, you can secure a training in the Humboldt State Normal School which will guarantee this result.

A very carefully planned course of study with full information concerning the school and its ideals is now ready for distribution.

With the enlarged faculty and the additional buildings and equipment, accommodations are provided for one hundred more students for the year, beginning August 2, 1916. Applications will be considered in the order in which they are received. Any application blank may be used.

Application Blanks and Course of Study can be secured by addressing President N.B. Van Matré, Arcata, California.

The Arcata Grammar School on 11th Street:
the original site of HSNS.

Humboldt State Normal in its infancy: the "shanghaied" football team; advanced orchestra, 1916; and (*opposite page*) classes in manual training, folk dancing and agriculture.

The student body elected its first officers in April of 1914: Leslie Graham, president; Joseph Crawford, vice president; Rhea Sage, secretary; Chester Carlson, treasurer. Loftus Gray served as athletic manager.

In the fine arts, students participated in the lyceum (sponsoring public entertainment), operas, chorale, glee club, orchestra, and dramatics.

The curtain rose on the school's first play, *Her Own Way*, December 3, 1914. Proceeds went to the Belgian Relief Fund in war-torn Europe. That performance, and many to follow, took place at the Minor Theatre. Such performances served as a bridge between the school and the community.

Among drama, music, student government, and athletics — teacher training still remained the school's primary focus. President Van Matré stressed,

> The course of study offered in the Humboldt State Normal School will make the very best teacher that it is possible to make out of those who enter.

As students moved through their probation for that profession, every aspect of their lives came under scrutiny. Men wore blue serge suits and white shirts. Women could wear no colors. "The greatest possible attention is given to the moral condition of these homes and communities in which the students live," said Van Matré. "Teaching school is and should be a very serious business." And so it was.

On May 26, 1915, the first graduating class participated in commencement ceremonies at the Minor Theatre. Fifteen women received certificates, including Susie Baker Fountain who, in December, 1914, became the first graduate. Arcatans in the class included Ana Averill Johnson, Grace May Bloomer Christensen, Ruth Mill Foltz, and Alice Jane

**Susie Baker Fountain,
the first graduate, 1914.**

Gale, daughter of trustee Charlotte Gale. The graduates were now qualified to teach elementary school.

"Pop" Jenkins

As the curriculum and student body expanded, so did the number of faculty. One new faculty member stands out: Horace "Pop" Jenkins, teacher of manual training for 38 years.

Some consider Jenkins the father of Humboldt's industrial arts program (though Emma Woodman actually preceded him in teaching it). Much of Pop Jenkins' influence came outside the classroom. For years he was known and loved for his doughnut and bean feeds, for taffy pulls after pep rallies and sporting events, and for his concern for students.

A New Campus

The growing school needed a new campus. Susie Baker Fountain called the grammar school site along the railroad tracks "irksome."

> Whenever the trains switched tracks, or the locomotives rumbled by, the building trembled and all classes came to a halt because of the noise.

The opportunity to move came available after the fall of 1914. William Preston and stockholders of the Union Water Company (directors: N.H. Falk, Len Yocum, Arthur Way, and Kate Harpst) donated 51 acres of the hilltop east of Arcata as a permanent site for HSNS. This included the present university site as well as lands east and north of today's campus.

14

The HSNS board of trustees accepted the gift and determined to construct temporary buildings on the Preston tract. The state provided $91,285 for the buildings, equipment, and salaries. Construction began in June, 1915.

One Arcata resident, Ana (Averell) Johnson, began her studies at the normal school in San Jose. She would travel there by steamer (aboard the Corona, the Pomona, or the Elder). In 1914 she transferred to the new Humboldt Normal School. By the spring of 1915, she had successfully completed the requirements to run a one-room schoolhouse. In anticipation of graduation day, each classmate was allotted $4.50 in material to make her own graduation gown in domestic science class.

from *The Lumberjack,* 1988

Temporary buildings were constructed of redwood, with pine floors. They were heated individually with wood stoves. Built in a quadrangle of 30 rooms, they occupied the site of what would become Founders Hall. To the south stood the gymnasium and library. To the east was the training school.

By January of 1916 the buildings were ready. Movers made the sloshy trek from Arcata Grammar School up the hill during one of the rainiest periods in history. Recorded rainfall that January totaled 13.02 inches, nearly four inches above the norm.

Hardly were the new buildings occupied before the president and others began appealing for a permanent building. Van Matré reported that the number of students had grown considerably in the school's two years (from 78 to 156) and that 381 students had now attended HSNS. He also reported that demand for student teaching had increased with the rising number of children attending the training school.

Student teachers, busy all week with the training school, had to attend classes on Saturdays now. (Until 1919, students had to practice teach seven different subjects to seven different grades, for 70 weeks!)

With additional community influence, the state legislature appropriated $245,000 to construct the new administration building. On the day Governor William Stevens signed the bill, June 2, 1917, nearly every resident of Arcata blew some kind of whistle or siren to celebrate. The *Arcata Union* reported a noise so impressive that some residents thought the World War had ended. This was not the case, unfortunately, and because of the war, construction of the permanent building would be delayed until 1920.

The War — & Local Battles
Against Declining Enrollment

On the third anniversary of the opening of Humboldt State Normal School, April 6, 1917, the U.S. entered World War I. The war would make a considerable impact on the school, nearly causing its demise.

HSNS enrollment, which reached a high of 159 in 1917, dropped to a low of 59 in 1920. Military service understandably caused a drastic decline in the male student population. Pop Jenkins complained of his manual arts class, "The workshop seems to produce nothing but hope chests. Still no men enrolled at Humboldt." Only two men enrolled in the fall of 1918.

Other factors contributed to the declining enrollment. A 1917 state law stiffened entrance requirements. No student could enter a normal school without a high school diploma, an 80 percent grade-point average, and a personal recommendation by her/his school principal.

Enrollment also declined as the teaching profession became less attractive because of higher-paying wartime jobs in business. A national teacher shortage between 1918 and 1921 suggests that low normal school enrollment occurred everywhere, not just at HSNS.

Economic hard times, which stretched across the nation in 1920-21, helped continue the downward trend. And locally, the fact that Humboldt State's costs for teacher training were higher than the costs at sister institutions in California ($291 per student at Santa Barbara, for example, compared with $753 per student at HSNS) only compounded the enrollment problems.

The state board of education considered retracting the money appropriated for the permanent building on the hilltop. They called the establishment of HSNS "a mistake." The intervention of Senator Hans Nelson helped prevent the nearly fatal retraction. Nonetheless, the board's misgivings held up the appropriation for the permanent building for nearly three years.

Meanwhile both school and community mounted strong efforts to recruit students. Extension courses by correspondence, introduced in 1917, allowed teachers in the field to gather units to qualify for a teaching certificate.

HSNS Letter, the school catalog, recruited both for HSNS and for the teaching profession in general. Between 1917 and 1919 the *Letter* featured specialty pictures and lesson plans to aid teachers of geography, spelling, and other courses. The catalog also touted the beauty of Arcata and the North Coast.

The original HSNS family, 1914

To show community support, civic organizations from Arcata and surrounding areas subscribed to a loan fund to assist HSNS students who needed financial aid.

The efforts barely succeeded, however. In 1919, a reported 500 schools in California needed teachers. It was not until after 1921, however, that normal school enrollment increased significantly, but that was probably due more to a return of improved economic conditions.

A New Name

The 1917 law revising admission standards also changed the administrative structure of state normal schools. Powers of the local trustees transferred to the state board of education. Normal school presidents could attend state board meetings and make requests, but the final word would now come from Sacramento. This represented a nationwide trend to standardize and consolidate decision making in matters of curriculum, textbooks, and admission and graduation requirements.

The HSNS board of eight years (including R.H. Edwards and Anna Porterfield who had joined original members Edward Haight, H.J. Bridges, and Rease Wiley) dissolved in 1921.

That was the year California made its normal schools into teachers colleges. San Jose, Chico, San Diego, San Francisco, Santa Barbara, Fresno, and Humboldt became a new system: the California State Teachers Colleges. Humboldt State Normal officially became Humboldt State Teachers College and Junior College. (Imagine spelling out HSTCJC across a letter sweater!)

Humboldt now offered a four-year teacher training course, planting the seed for an eventual bachelor's degree in education. Humboldt also offered a two-year junior college program that would transfer toward a B.A. at the University of California.

The school broadened its course offerings considerably. More and more, Humboldt's courses were oriented toward subject-matter general education. Manual training, for instance, was no longer required of every student. Economics, biology, and other subjects took its place.

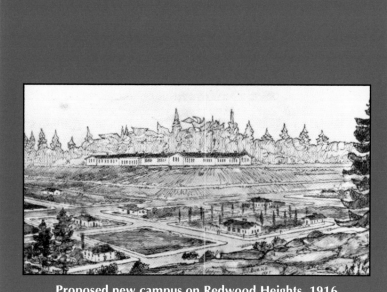

Proposed new campus on Redwood Heights, 1916

Survival Summary

Worthwhile (and not-so-worthwhile) endeavors sometimes end almost as soon as they've begun. There are no guarantees. The first seven years of Humboldt State were significant if for no other reason than that the fledgling school surmounted a number of obstacles and survived.

The Swimmin' Hole

Athletics and physical education received a small boost in the postwar years. Workers began developing a leveled athletic field in the canyon east of the temporary buildings on the hilltop (present site of Redwood Bowl).

Sometimes they worked on an athletic field. On other occasions they developed that area with visions of a picnic and recreational area. Either way, most of the visible results would have to wait until the 30s.

A "swimmin' hole" splashed onto the scene in 1920. While an outdoor pool in a North Coast climate did little for student recruitment, William Preston had specified that a swimming pool be built on the property he granted HSNS. Workers constructed an eight-foot concrete wall to hold back water from a stream above Jolly Giant Canyon just north of today's Redwood Bowl.

According to Coach Joseph Forbes,

> This pool, fed by spring water from the stream, combined with the freezing temperature of the air, discouraged all but the most (fool)hardy.

Despite shaky beginnings (and even shakier facilities) at Arcata Grammar School and up on the hilltop, despite a world war, despite institutional reorganization and economic hard times, Humboldt State entered the 20s with bright prospects for its future.

Symbolic of that spirit of optimism and endurance: construction had begun on the new administration building, the future Founders Hall.

Some attribute Humboldt's survival into the 20s to the leadership of President Van Matré or to the support and dedication of faculty members and students. It was the outside community, however, that cemented the structure.

Citizens of Arcata and outlying communities gave money, time, moral and political support to ensure the survival of their school. They pledged funds and facilities to get HSNS off the ground in 1913-14. They organized to find room and board for students. Several donated land for a permanent site. They established a loan fund for students. They lobbied in Sacramento to ensure support for the normal at the state level. Without such community support, HSNS would have closed its doors before 1920.

A
Tribute
to "Pop"

He's been described as "almost Christlike . . . the sweetest, gentlest man." Ruth Chapman, a student in the 20s, remembers, "Everybody loved him, whether you were in his classes or not." Gayle Karshner remembers him during the World War II years as being very sensitive to people's needs, especially those whose loved ones had gone overseas.

A temporary shack thrown up during World War I became Pop's Shop, the center for his industrial arts classes and, judging by many students' memories, a makeshift kitchen where he often fed his students. He had a large iron pot like a witch's kettle with an open fire underneath. In and after class, he cooked candy, soups, and beans which — during the Depression — comprised the only hot meal of the day for some students.

Pop also taught toy-making and pottery classes. One of his friends remembers the time he and his class constructed a boat inside what is now Jenkins Hall. They either built the boat too big, or the architects designed the building too small because a concrete wall had to be removed in order to get the boat out.

Pop and his wife Anna were blessed with two sons. One son, Channing, a reconnaissance photographer over Normandy in World War II, was killed the day before D-Day. Pop got the news while on a cross-country train. Later he would claim it was in that moment that the Parkinson's disease (which eventually crippled him) began invading his body. After the war, however, Pop received the surprising news that Channing had gotten married during the war. His English war bride came to America and presented Pop with his new grandson (see photo). This was joyous news to a man so deserving — a man who, himself, had given so much joy.

Pop Jenkins as a young man (*left*) and with his grandson, Channing, on the cover of a *Humboldt Hilarities* program.

(clockwise from top right) The Minor Theatre, corner of 10th & H Streets, where the first HSNS commencement took place; graduates wearing gowns they made; opening night at Pettengill's Minor Theatre, Dec. 3, 1914; Mr. Beer and son in potato patch on President Van Matré's lot, present site of the art building.

(*center*) In the background is the first HSNS building on the Preston tract; (*top and bottom*) Early stages of construction of the administration building (later called Founders Hall), completed in 1922.

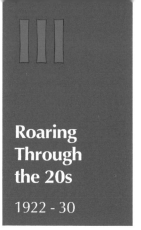
Like most colleges, Humboldt State Teachers College experienced growth and prosperity in the years just preceding the Great Depression. Enrollment, faculty, and curriculum expanded. Extracurricular activities flourished. The physical layout of the campus improved. The 20s roared for Humboldt State.

A Permanent Home

The early months of 1922 saw the campus' first permanent building completed atop Preston Ridge. It was called the Main Building or Administration Building until renamed Founders Hall in 1959.

This structure housed classrooms, faculty and administrative offices, a library, and an auditorium. The east wing served as the training school for elementary school teachers. Thirty-nine arches and doorways remained open air until 1927. In her written account, historian Sarah Davies recalled, "Students found the permanent building much less comfortable before these arches were enclosed."

When Humboldt joined the California State Teachers Colleges system in 1921, the local board lost its official status. Before disbanding, however, the trustees and a group of local businesspersons saw to it that the redwood quadrangle of temporary buildings hastily erected in late 1915 was put to good use.

Presidential secretary Martha Beer Roscoe witnessed the quadrangle's piece-by-piece transportation down the hill for use in a 50-person dormitory on the site of present-day Nelson Hall. Then, as one of their last acts, the trustees

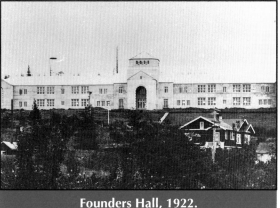

Founders Hall, 1922.

authorized construction of a cafeteria south of the main building.

The 20s would also see a new red tile roof on the main building (1925), a bookstore at its entrance (1923), and land purchases for a future gymnasium and tennis courts.

A Growing Enrollment

Humboldt coordinated its efforts to recruit and retain students. The college catalog, *Circular of Information,* stressed the appeal of the natural environment: redwoods, lumber camps, the coastline, and "a succession of wonderful panoramas in which Humboldt Bay holds the center of the picture."

The school also used new summer sessions in its recruiting spiel. Both prospective teachers and employed, noncertified teachers could take advantage of Humboldt's mild summer climate to earn elementary teaching certificates and state credentials. To raise money to advertise this fact, Humboldt students presented dramatic performances of *The Arrival of Kitty* in 1925. The play brought in a thousand dollars and, indirectly, a number of new students.

Enrollment tripled during the decade, peaking at 372 in 1930. Men students, still a minority, constituted one third of that total. Nearly three students in four came from the North Coast.

The physical act of arriving on campus — a city set upon a hill — seldom proved easy. Esma Catherine (Duck) Hunt, a 1924 graduate, testified to the limited transportation facilities.

(clockwise from top right) **Courtyard of the new building (Founders Hall), 1922; "temporary" buildings on south end; main entrance; copy of "Winged Victory" in main lobby.**

22

"Four students had cars," she recalled. Her daily commute from Eureka began "around the bay by train, to be met by a Model T at the siding at the foot of the hill for transporting up the grade."

Students needing a job obtained part-time employment on campus. (Room and board for dormitory residents cost $24 per month in 1925. Registration and student body fees were $1.50 and $5, respectively.) At the other end of the educational process, a placement service helped graduates obtain teaching positions.

Homer Balabanis

New Curriculum, New Faculty

The primary academic mission of the college remained teacher training, but new secondary purposes accompanied the transition to teachers college/junior college status.

A Junior Certificate prepared high school graduates for further education through two years of "federal foundation" courses which would transfer to the University of California. Humboldt State also offered more vocational training, including an auto and tractor mechanics course and a two-year commercial course.

Academic programs opened up to allow for diversity and electives. Foreign languages expanded to include French, Spanish, Latin, and German. Lower division offerings expanded in the fields of hygiene, physical education, mathematics, natural science, English, philosophy, and the social sciences. So great was the expansion, that by 1926 the college received authorization to offer a B.A. degree. Four years later a bachelor's degree was required of everyone in teacher training.

The changes in academic programs meant new faculty. While the 1921-22 catalog listed 16 faculty members, with Pop Jenkins the senior member, that number would nearly double by the time of the stock market crash in late 1929. Several familiar names appear on the faculty and administration lists: Jessie Turner Woodcock, secretary to the

president, registrar, and treasurer in the early years; Homer Balabanis, who arrived in 1923 to teach French, economics, and sociology; Fred Telonicher, men's athletic coach; Laura Herron, women's coach; Imogene Platt, registrar, 1926; Leo Schussman, head of the department of education; Maurice Hicklin, English and journalism professor; and Edward and Emily Graves, librarians.

End of the Van Matré Era

President Van Matré served until 1924, and was succeeded by Ralph Swetman. Van Matré is credited with helping Humboldt survive that first difficult and parsimonious decade. By the time he left, Humboldt was a permanent fixture in the California State Teachers Colleges system.

Homer Balabanis attributed the school's heavy stress on moral character to Van Matré. His was a noble, purposive vision for the teaching profession. By the strength of his convictions, however, he wielded strong control over student and faculty lives, including their social behavior. He could hire and fire faculty members at his discretion. Balabanis noted:

> It has been alleged that faculty turnover was high because the president did not want any faculty member to earn sufficient tenure to challenge his authority.

Indeed, the popular Pop Jenkins was let go by Van Matré for the 1923-24 academic year. Fortunately for Humboldt students, President Swetman rehired Jenkins in 1924.

President Swetman

Ralph Swetman made notable contributions to Humboldt during his six-year tenure. His efforts to repair relations between Arcata and Eureka succeeded, in large part. Though

23

Helen Stover began her schooling in 1925, climbing wooden sidewalks to the College Elementary School in Founders Hall. By the time she graduated 8th grade, CES occupied Gist Hall. Four years later she returned, along with many of her classmates, this time for a college education.

Students of CES were those who lived in the area, though some were from Eureka and environs. Some were children of local educators (Helen's father was Professor Homer Arnold), while still others — the "incorrigible" and slow learners — were sent from Arcata Grammar School to get special attention. Classes were small. Most Arcatans sent their children to Arcata Grammar, considering CES "too permissive." But Stover believes their school was more enlightened, with students' individuality taken seriously.

A study unit on Japan, for instance, involved a Japanese tea and an exchange of dolls with the emperor's daughter. Stella Little, from the college faculty, taught them watercolors. Professor Marie Ostrander taught second graders to sightread music and sing parts. After lunch, Mrs. Ostrander played records while students costumed themselves in theatrical props and free-danced to the music. The kids could use the college library. Former student, Jean Falor, (Professor Schussman's daughter), recalls picking wild strawberries on the hill. In addition, students had strong instruction (by Humboldt's student teachers and their supervisors) in reading, grammar, and math.

Only occasionally did all this freedom backfire. Professor MacGinitie let two boys (one was Helen Stover's brother) into his chemistry lab to satisfy their curiosity about making gunpowder. When the boys were late back to class, the teacher confiscated their package and set it on the corner of her desk — which just happened to be up against a hot radiator. You can guess the rest.

Second grade in Founders Hall, 1929-30.

many Eurekans still fostered hard feelings over the location of the normal school, Swetman cultivated better relations by participating in many service clubs and organizations. He gave speeches, attended city functions, and recruited students. He induced the *Humboldt Times* and the *Arcata Union* to cooperate in promoting better relations between the two cities and the college.

Arcata businessmen took an important step in promoting college and community relations in 1928, when they founded the HSTC Improvement Association. Members of that group included H.W. Jackson, S.D. Cerini, Ralph Bull, J.J. Krohn, Vernon Hunt, Henry Brizard, Frank Tooby, and George Averell.

The association bought land for the site of the College Elementary School (now Gist Hall) and raised funds to improve the dormitories. An offspring of that organization, the HSU Foundation, continues to this day as a symbol of strong university/community relations.

Meanwhile, Swetman raised academic standards at Humboldt by introducing a grade-point average system, an academic probation system, and an honor roll. He also raised qualifications for full-time faculty members:

1) possession of an M.A. or Ph.D. from a recognized university;

President Ralph Swetman

2) a major in the discipline taught, with a minor in education or psychology;

3) a willingness to teach elementary grades or extension courses for adults;

4) a constructive, optimistic, enthusiastic, and kindly attitude;

5) motivation to do some study or investigation in either the major field or in education;

6) a commitment to progressive education founded on scientific thinking.

The president adhered to the popular idea of child-centered education touted at Columbia Teachers College and Stanford University. As historian Sarah Davies put it:

President Swetman was called an apostle — a crusader for the child's rights. He approached the work of training teachers with missionary zeal.

Swetman also loved outdoor recreation and hiking. Librarian Edward Graves declared the president was so enthusiastic about the redwood forest east of Humboldt that he "personally took up axe and mattock to help make a trail through it."

Athletics

The president's attitude no doubt promoted greater emphasis on athletics and physical education during the 20s. These were days of national sports heroes such as boxers Jack Dempsey and Gene Tunney, and football's Four Horsemen of Norte Dame. At Humboldt, the "household names" were coaches Bert Smith, Fred Falkenberg, Fred Telonicher, and Laura Herron; and student athletes Bill Pederson, Leo Sullivan, and (especially) Elta Cartwright.

Former professor and coach Joseph Forbes and former athlete Janet Ferguson have written competent but unpublished histories of athletics at Humboldt. These works suggest four highlights in sports during the 20s:

*U*pon his retirement, Professor Hicklin explained his decision to come to Humboldt: "I was studying at Stanford University, intending to stay until I got my doctorate, when I was offered the position on HSC's faculty in 1925. I came up to visit and found the scenery so beautiful, and the people in the town and the college so friendly, that the first thing I knew, I'd been here 31 years!"

1) the ministering of activities which had shifted to the student body in 1924;

2) the creation of the Women's Athletic Association in 1925, and the subsequent hiring of Laura Herron;

3) the phenomenal success of women's athletics, capped by Elta Cartwright's participation in the 1928 Olympics;

4) the first intercollegiate football contest in 1927.

Women's Athletics & "Cinder" Elta

Women athletes brought expansion and honor to Humboldt's athletic programs. Laura Herron, who had taught physical education at Eureka High School, came to Humboldt State in 1925. For the next five years she organized a highly successful program for women.

Herron initiated the campus Women's Athletic Association and the Humboldt County branch of the Northern California Athletic Association (1927). Her athletes competed both inside and outside Humboldt County. She achieved a high degree of participation in intramural athletics, fielding teams in volleyball, field hockey, basketball, softball, track and field, and tennis. In 1925 she organized Play Day — a day of sports on campus for local high school girls. This became an annual event for many years.

The 20s roared for women's athletics. At one track and field practice meet in 1926, Coach Herron's women beat the Humboldt State *men* 33 to 26! The women's basketball team traveled through Mendocino County, and played several high school teams. These activities received strong presidential support. (He might have shown less enthusiasm had he known the whole story. Former Humboldt athlete Bernice Stokes Harpst recalled, "We met many boys and girls from these areas, broke training rules, partied around after the coach was in bed, and really had a good time.")

In speaking of Humboldt's women athletes, the brightest spotlight certainly must fall on track star "Cinder" Elta Cartwright. In 1926 she helped her team win a national track meet in San Francisco. In 1927 "Cinder" Elta tied the women's world record in the 100 yard dash (11.4 seconds) and set a new world record in the women's broad jump. In 1928 she was the first woman selected for America's first Women's Olympic Team, which competed in Amsterdam.

Coach Laura Herron had turned around women's athletics at Humboldt. Yet despite her success as coach and promoter, her personal habits were not to the liking of President Swetman. He let her go. Homer Balabanis related that she was "too independent for Swetman, and she smoked cigarettes." Jessie Turner Woodcock, even more explicit, said, "People reported her for having students in her home, drinking, and all kinds of wild parties going on . . . I even went to one of the wild parties."

Whatever the case, from Herron's departure until the 60s, women's athletics would exist largely on a local and intramural level at Humboldt. Still, participation and support remained strong.

Men's Athletics

Men's athletics boasted far less success than the women's programs during the 20s. Between 1923 and 1927, coaches Bert Smith and Fred Falkenberg arranged for the baseball, basketball, and football teams to play Northern California high school and amateur teams. The school promoted sporting events more as recruiting tools to attract more men to Humboldt State.

The shortage of male students proved a persistent hindrance to athletics. For example, the football team disbanded in 1926 when several players' academic ineligibility decimated the squad. *Cabrillo*, the 1927 yearbook, noted grimly:

> For the second time in the history of the school, Humboldt experimented with football, and for the second time in its history found the game too much for it.

Elta Cartwright's Olympic Summer

Source:
The Humboldt Times,
July 5 - August 29, 1928

In the summer of 1928, Babe Ruth was belting homers every few days, Johnny Weismuller ("Tarzan") was breaking swimming records, and Herbert Hoover was camping at Bull Creek. But it was a diminutive 20-year old HSTC graduate, Elta Cartwright, who was capturing the hearts of Northern Californians and much of the nation.

On July 4, coach Laura Herron's Northern California Athletic Club dominated the national track meet in Newark. Elta won the 50 yard dash, 100 meter dash, and broad jump, leading one national wire service to proclaim her "the outstanding woman athlete in the US."

Seven days later Elta boarded the *President Roosevelt,* chartered for the American team's passage to the Amsterdam Olympics. The 10-day voyage was difficult. Team members endured sea-sickness, severely limited training facilities, and a distressing incident in which a crew member, thrown in the brig for drunkenness, accidentally set himself afire and died.

In Amsterdam, Elta reached the semifinals in the 100 meter dash before being eliminated. Gracious in defeat, she made no alibis. "I gave all I could," she wrote home. "I only hope that the people of Humboldt do not think I was unworthy of the trip ... Miss Herron gave me a lovely bunch of pink roses for a consolation prize. A little note tied to the roses read: 'In defeat as in victory. Laura.' Last night I ran that race over 50 times in my sleep. But when I woke up and saw my consolation prize, I realized the darn race was really over."

The hearts of North Coasters went out to their champion. Eureka's chamber of commerce planned a welcoming celebration for Elta and her teammates, anticipating a crowd of 2,000. As the *Humboldt Times* recorded, "An entire county turned out to pay homage to its athletic heroines and welcomed them home with a celebration such as has never been equaled in Eureka."

As many as 15,000 people lined the streets for the parade. Hundreds more greeted Elta's bunting-bedecked train at every stop between Sausalito and Fields Landing. They waved flags and banners. Sirens blew, bands played and children sang. Never before—and perhaps not since — had Humboldt witnessed such a whole-hearted outpouring of love. All for a modest young teachers-college graduate who would, within the week, trade in her key to the city for a key to a small classroom in Petrolia.

(clockwise)
Aerial view of
20s campus with
women's dorm
on left and many
private homes;
ukulele ensem-
ble,1927;"Kids'"
party, 1922;
Women's Ath-
letic Association,
1927.

Basketball teams found slightly more success. They competed in the Humboldt County Independent League, composed of local amateur teams sporting such colorful names as the Samoa Bluedevils and the Hollander (Eureka) Sparklers.

Humboldt played its first intercollegiate football game in the fall of 1927. Newly arrived coach and biology professor, Fred Telonicher, took his team of 12 men to play at Southern Oregon Normal School in Ashland. They lost 33-0. Still, it was a first. Under Telonicher's tutelage, Humboldt continued to engage in intercollegiate play with Southern Oregon, Chico State, and others. The first football victory came in 1929 against San Francisco College of Pharmacy.

HSTC Band, 1927.

*M*ore than just a long-time coach of the football and basketball teams, Fred Telonicher was also an excellent teacher. Students from his physiology classes went on to excel at Cal and various medical schools. Humboldt gained a strong reputation for its pre-med program.

Stars of the men's athletic teams of the 20s included Bill Pederson, Leo Sullivan, Abner Brantley, and basketball captain Ben Feuerwerker.

Associated Students

Associated Students of the Humboldt State Teachers College and Junior College was founded in the fall of 1924 to create student self-government, promote athletics, cooperate with faculty, establish ideals of honesty and fair play in every phase of student life, and nurture a feeling of loyalty to [the] school.

The first AS officers were Howard Trueblood, president, and Monroe Spaght, vice president. The constitution also provided for athletic managers for both men and women. For more than two decades, the athletic managers helped coaches gain resources for athletic programs.

The Student Community

In many ways the organizations and activities on and off campus created a sense of community and promoted attendance at Humboldt State. To participate in extracurricular activities, students had to carry at least ten semester units of passing course work, attend classes regularly, and pay student body dues. A five-student board of control monitored "standards of proper conduct and honorable scholarship."

Students lacked no opportunity for participation, especially in the musical and performing arts. Seventy-five students and faculty put on a 12-act comedy, *The College Jinx,* in 1924 to raise money for lamps in front of the main building. A 1925 play, *Slates,* starred Estelle Preston and Monroe Spaght.

The College Lyceum, later called The Collegians, presented musical and dramatic programs both on campus and in various communities along the North Coast. The Lyceum featured a jazz orchestra, the Melody Men, who performed in a radio broadcast from San Francisco in 1930. One of their favorite numbers was "Moonlight and Roses."

Monroe Spaght

One of the school's distinguished alumni, Monroe Spaght, was a local boy who began attending HSTC at the age of only 14. (He had entered Arcata Union High School at age 10.)

Despite his youth, Spaght was a "big man on campus" during the mid-20s. He appeared in dramatic productions, played trombone solos with the college orchestra (which in those days primarily played popular dance tunes), served as the first vice president of Associated Students, and acted as toastmaster for banquets.

After three years at Humboldt, Spaght transferred to Stanford where he completed his bachelor's, master's and doctoral degrees. He then joined Shell Oil Company as a research chemist, working his way up the corporate ladder until he became president in 1960. Later, he became managing director of the Royal Dutch Petroleum Company.

In his later philanthropic efforts, Spaght never forgot his North Coast alma mater. Most notably, he established a distinguished lecturer series that continues to bring prominent business leaders to campus. In appreciation, the alumni association honored Spaght with the Who's Who award during the school's Golden Anniversary celebration in 1963.

What else? All-college dances, lectures, class parties, a Cosmopolitan Club, and the Audubon Bird Club. Associated Women Students involved students and faculty in a Big Sister/Little Sister program through which "better study habits were formed, more acquaintances were made, and cliques were eliminated."

Work Day, initiated in 1925, quickly became a popular and useful activity. With classes called off, all students and faculty cleaned up the campus buildings and grounds. The work gave way to a party and dance in the evening, a tradition that endured until 1956.

We Have Alumni Now

Indicative of Humboldt State's increasing stability and institutional maturity, 1924 saw the formation of an alumni association. The first officers were Hugh Stewart, president; Emily Duprey Murray, vice president; and Jessie Turner Woodcock, secretary.

The association sponsored the school's first homecoming, honoring the not-so-distant class of 1917. A football game with Arcata High (9-0 in favor of Humboldt) preceded a gathering of students, faculty, and alumni at the Arcata Fireman's Hall.

Literary Pursuits

Among other "firsts" during the 20s were student publications.

Students published a yearbook, *Cabrillo,* in 1927. (The Spanish navigator Cabrillo, blown off course in 1542, was perhaps the first European to set foot on the North Coast.)

The yearbook had class photographs, informal snapshots, and special sections on extracurricular activities during the 1926-27 school year. Photographs of faculty members included Homer Arnold, education; Homer Balabanis, social science; Maurice Hicklin, English and journalism; Laura Herron, physical education; Horace "Pop" Jenkins, industrial arts; Leo Schussman, education; and the president's secretary, Jessie Turner Woodcock.

The first student newspaper, appropriately named *The Foghorn*, went to press during the 1924-25 school year. Edited by Lee Baird, it featured short stories, special columns, and news notes. Students assessed themselves a $6 fee in the spring of 1925, but their support proved insufficient to keep the paper going.

The next effort to publish a student newspaper came in 1929. Lawrence Morris edited *HSTC Rooter* (to indicate its purpose as a booster of the college). One year later students renamed it *The Lumberjack*, which has survived to this day. At that time, Associated Students, not the journalism department, published the newspaper.

Early issues of the *Rooter* contained book reviews of current best sellers, poetry, and articles on sports and school spirit. There were also vigorous debates on prohibition, student government, "100 percent Americanism," proposed fines for class absences, women smoking, world peace, and other issues of local and national interest. The paper featured a scandal column and interesting attempts at humor: "I call my girl 'gravity' because she is so attractive."

Perhaps the most momentous news for Humboldt Staters appeared in a January, 1930, banner headline: "DR. SWETMAN RESIGNS!"

The Faculty Wives

The Faculty Wives organization began in the days when the fish man drove the streets of Arcata each Friday, honking his horn and selling fresh fish (the crab) to the housewives. Some of the faculty wives — Margaret Telonicher, Frances Balabanis, Martha Hicklin, Bea MacGinitie, Hazel Jeffers, Elma Arnold, Bonnie Wilson, Ruth Gist, and others — chose Fridays to have crab lunch together. Calling themselves the Crab and Culture Society, they'd visit, sew, and enjoy book reports or short programs. A few years later, the group would evolve into the Faculty Wives — an organization that existed up until the 70s.

Meeting of the Crab and Culture Society, late 20s (*front row l-r*) Henrietta Schussman, Martha Hicklin, Anna Jenkins; (*back row l-r*) Emily Graves, Mrs. Balcomb, and Alice Swetman.

The Humboldt Lyceum

Sources: *Humboldt State Normal Bulletin, Cabrillo, Humboldt Times*

The original Lyceum was the Athenian gymnasium Aristotle used as a classroom. By the turn of the century, *lyceum* had come to signify any association providing lectures, concerts, or public entertainment. From its earliest years, HSNS took great pride in the quality of its lyceum programs — five per year — at Arcata's Minor Theatre.

From 1925 to 1930, Humboldt took its show on the road, both as a service to outlying communities and as a recruiting campaign. The lyceum featured small orchestras, vocal and instrumental soloists, one-act comedies ("Freezing a Mother-in-Law," for instance), opera scenes, dramatic monologues (Virginia Herron starred), brass quartets, ukulele choruses, ballet and jazz dancers — even acrobats (brother and sister Ronald and Ione, The Tumbling Russells).

They were a huge success. They played the hot spots in Crescent City, Orick, Crannell, Korbel, Blue Lake, Ferndale, Fortuna, Scotia, Garberville, Willitts, Lakeport, Ukiah, Sebastopol, Petaluma, Santa Rosa, and Vallejo. They even had a radio appearance on KPO, San Francisco. The 1926 tour reached over 5,000 people. The 1929 troupe, now called The Humboldt Collegians, played to a record 1,675 in two nights at the Minor Theatre.

The lyceum did much to establish HSTC's reputation as a cultural center for the North Coast.

The
Social Circuit

Source:
1927 Cabrillo

Home Economics Tea

Residents of Arcata and vicinity were invited to a tea given at the college Friday afternoon, August 26, from 3:20 to 5:15 in the new college cafeteria. Dancing was enjoyed and a program was given.

Christmas Dance

In December, 1926, a Christmas dance was held in the library. The decorations were very attractive and in keeping with the season. A novel feature was the snowstorm showered on the dancers at intervals during the evening. Punch was served during the evening.

Literati Banquet

A dinner and initiation were held in the social unit of the college Thursday, January 27, 1927. A one-act play was presented during the evening and a dance number was given.

San Jose Banquet

On February 4, the Associated Men Students of the College gave a banquet for the San Jose basketball team and the firemen team. Monroe Spaght acted as toastmaster. During the banquet a program was given.

Cosmopolitan Club

Thursday, February 17, the Cosmopolitan Club held its first social meeting of the year. Ben Feuerwerker was toastmaster at the banquet, held in the social unit of the college at 6 o'clock. A program was presented after dinner and an interesting talk given by President Ralph W. Swetman.

Mardi Gras Dinner Dance

The cafeteria and dormitory entertained the student body at a costume ball February 25, 1927. Dinner was served at 6:30, with dancing between courses. After the dinner, dancing was enjoyed until 12 o'clock. Elenore Yocom reigned as queen and Truman Wood as king.

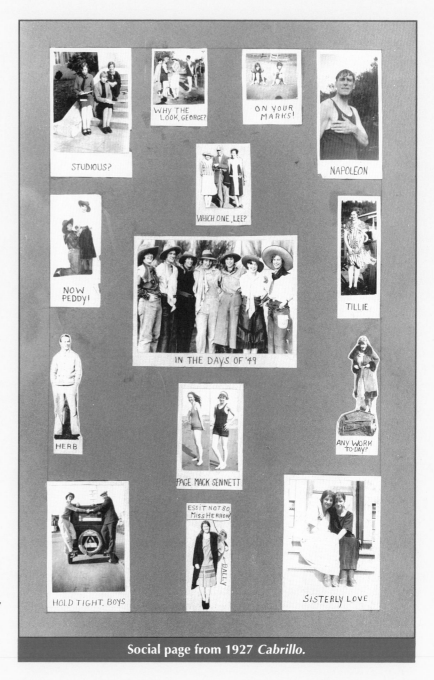

Social page from 1927 *Cabrillo*.

**First Letter
Home
July, 1927**

*D*ear Adorable Family:

At last my journey is end-ed, and I am a student in this far-away College, — I might almost say, this College in the country. But let me begin at the beginning.

First to preserve this at-mosphere of remoteness, after a long walk from the stage depot, one arrives at the foot of a hill, upon which the school is lo-cated. It is true, is it not, that gaining an education *is* "up-hill" work? But

reaching the foot of the stairs leading to the en-trance, I patiently — a step at a time — counted to forty-four before I found myself within the building. Good fortune at-tended me for there stood a most efficient-looking lady, of whom I quickly inquired my way to the Girls' Dormitory. In a most businesslike manner she replied — "Right down the hill; first detour to the right."

It will seem strange to you that having just ascended that hill, I had failed to recognize my future home, but wait —

I now proceeded to fol-low directions, made the detour, and found myself confronted by a low ram-bling structure, quaint and picturesque. It is hard

to tell you just the style — one needs the ability to write descriptive prose, for it is so "fetching." Ap-proaching the building, there came to me sounds as of the stroke of an axe. You know how poems al-ways come to me. Imme-diately I thought of those lines — "Woodman, spare that tree." Instinctively my steps quickened. Now, what do you suppose it was: — <u>Only a Dormitory girl chopping kindling</u>. Isn't that too thrilling!

I have since learned that every girl learns to use an ax. What a magnificent opportunity to develop energy — initiative — poise!! It brought to my mind a subject for some future theme, such as Physical Independence — or Advantages of Dormi-tory Life — or — Wood-pile Anthropology. Such a lot of ideas came trip-ping along.

You will want to know about my room, (I will describe it in detail later)

but it is _so lofty_, making one feel that here is a place conducive to high _thinking_. And the windows open out in most enticing fashion. Any young man passing by would want to step up for a chat. (I was so disappointed to find that this is not allowed.) But it gives one such a romantic feeling. "Gaily, the troubadour" — you know.

Then the laundry. Keeping up the fire there is something like a relay race, each one in turn carrying wood. Another

chance, you see, to gain physical prowess. Speaking in terms of the movies, one might call it "a continuous performance."

And now, — about our lawn. Seldom does one see grass grow so luxuriantly as it does here. It attains such a height that it may be dignified by being called hay. Do you know, I mean to tell the girls what a fine chance for dramatization this will furnish. You remember that old poem, "Maud Muller on a summer day/ Raked the meadow sweet

with hay." The girls would be so sweet with picture hats and lovely new rakes. Don't I think of more things, folks? There is certainly something about this climate that sharpens one's wits. There surely can be no dullards in this school.

The best comes last — _Our dear social room_. It does not contain the type of furniture so commonly used now. No overstuffed davenport, and such things. Every — piece — is — so different. Even the piano has an individuality of its own, being, in color, a cheerful red. These things, I'm sure, belong to different periods, but all border on the antique. It fairly takes one back.

Now the girls — they

speak for themselves, as you would agree if you could only hear them. You shall at least _hear more about them_.

There's the whistle from the athletic field. It just occurs to me what a double opportunity one has, with both natural and artificial athletics. But I must hurry to school. Now isn't California wonderful — wonderful! It's truly unusual, folks!

Your affectionate and happy

Mary Lou Humboldt

"Estelle Preston McDowell and her family are extremely important in the history of Humboldt State University. When Estelle was younger, the Preston House was located near where our library now stands. The Preston orchard stood where there is now library parking. The Preston House had a magnificent view of the bay.

"It was Estelle's father, William A. Preston, who gave the original land upon which Humboldt State was founded in 1913. There was a great rivalry between Arcata and Eureka for the university. There was a good deal of lobbying in Sacramento before Humboldt State finally was located in Arcata. Estelle can remember the day her dad came running in the door yelling, 'We got it! We got it!'

"After attending Humboldt State from 1924-26, Estelle taught for 12 years in Sacramento County. She returned to Humboldt to serve as a demonstration teacher in the College Elementary School on campus. Later she served on the board of directors for the HSU Alumni Association, and became president of that organization. In 1964 Estelle and her husband Robert donated the [three]-acre site for our Redwood Sciences Building [today's Pacific Southwest Forest and Range Experiment Station].

"It is with great pride and pleasure that I introduce to you our 1983 homecoming queen, Estelle Preston McDowell. . . ."

The Depression Years:

the 1930s

The 1929 crash of the New York Stock Exchange precipitated an unparalleled national economic crisis — the Great Depression — for nearly ten years. At the same time, tensions were rising worldwide. Dictators rose to power in Italy, Germany, and Japan. Acts of aggression in Manchuria, Ethiopia, China, and Eastern Europe pointed toward the world war that would break out in September of 1939.

President Gist

Guiding Humboldt State through these difficult years was new president Arthur Gist, who replaced Ralph Swetman in the fall of 1930. (Swetman had accepted the presidency of Arizona State Teachers College in Tempe.)

President Arthur Gist

Gist brought to Humboldt a great enthusiasm for teacher training. He had B.S. and M.A. degrees in education from the University of Washington. He had served as an elementary school principal in both Washington and California and as director of teacher education at San Francisco State Teachers College.

Gist viewed schools as prominent agents for improving society: promoting awareness of social issues, for instance. He allowed faculty and students more say in school governance as part of their citizenship training. Gist also promoted the cause of increased professionalism among teachers, a strong trend during the 30s.

Besides his passion for education, Gist possessed strong people skills. The new president proved himself solicitous of individual students. He would serve informal breakfasts and dinners to small groups of students, especially freshmen. He would help them get jobs. Ugo Giuntini and Oden Hansen, 30s graduates, credit Gist with arranging their first jobs at a time when teaching positions — jobs in general — were scarce.

Gist took an avid interest in building good college/community relations. Two examples: he helped found both the Northern California Guidance Association (made up of public school administrators and counselors) and the Community Concert Association (sponsor of musical performances in Eureka and other North Coast communities).

All these attributes would prove invaluable to the college in an age of rising tensions and dwindling hopes, an age when, as Jessie Turner Woodcock (HSTC comptroller in 1930) recalled,

> We just couldn't have *anything*. State revenues were reduced, and it was local people — business people — who helped keep the college afloat.

Hard Times

The Depression manifested itself in many ways on campus. The initial crunch came in 1932-33, with a rise in tuition from $1.50 to $6.50 per semester. This led spring pre-registration students to submit IOUs in place of fee payments, a practice eliminated by the state the following fall.

Although the per-student budget decreased from $371 to $314, students, faculty, and community members struggled just to keep the doors open. The state threatened to close down three teachers colleges, including Humboldt, for lack of funds. President Gist had to hurry to Sacramento to talk the board of education out of such a drastic measure.

Back home, in a scramble to boost enrollment, Senior Day brought local high school students to campus. Faculty wives sponsored a Poverty Ball in 1933 and established a student loan fund. The community helped wherever it could. Later in the decade, federal monies from the Federal Emergency Relief Act and the Civil Works Administration provided campus employment for students and others.

At Home with the Gists

In the small, "family" days of HSC, President Gist was friends with many students — indeed he knew each one. He had lunch in the Nelson Hall cafeteria nearly every day. Well-known for his witty stories, he often started college assemblies with the line, "I feel like a mummy — pressed for time."

His wife Ruth, who had a delightful sense of humor, was well-known as a speaker throughout the county. She entertained constantly, both formally and informally, in her home on campus (where the science buildings now stand).

Once a year she brought together campus and community by inviting a large number of county residents to her home for a reception to meet the new faculty. At an annual Christmas party for faculty children, she would lean the leaves of the dining room table against the big window seat in the living room, to provide a slide for the toddlers.

At informal parties, guests would gather around the piano to sing songs from the teens, 20s, and 30s. Sometimes the guest list would include performers from the community concerts in Eureka, including one memorable evening with Gregor Piatigorsky.

By December, 1933, the greatest crisis had passed. President Gist stated: "I feel that the friends of Humboldt State have been successful in their efforts to save the college." Humboldt State celebrated its 20th anniversary on April 6, 1934.

Despite Hard Times . . .

Despite the economic shortfall and hard times for faculty and students alike, Humboldt State endured. In fact, enrollment increased steadily; the curriculum expanded; physical facilities improved; and in 1935 the school underwent a second name change, reflective of a broader sense of purpose: Humboldt State College.

Enrollment did dip from 372 in 1930-31, to 286 in 1931-32. But after threat of closure in 1932, the college introduced pre-registration for the fall terms. From then on, enrollment grew steadily, reaching 424 in 1939-40. The increase, in part, accompanied the shortage of jobs for young people. A rise in University of California admission standards also contributed, as did a renewed emphasis on vocational education. A majority of the students came from Humboldt County, and more than two-thirds from the North Coast.

While enrollment increased, the size of the faculty remained between 28 and 30. To meet curricular needs, instructors had to teach quite a variety of courses. Education professor Homer Arnold, during a 12-year period, taught 31 courses, from arithmetic to philosophy (far different from our present emphasis on specialization).

Campus Changes

The campus took on a new look during this period. The old gymnasium south of the main building (now Founders Hall) gave way to a new gym to the southeast. It was dedicated in March of 1931 on the occasion of President Gist's formal inauguration.

Builders completed the new College Elementary School in 1933, a favored project of Gist. The school no longer functions as he envisioned, but the building still stands and rightfully bears his name today.

In 1937 a cooperative bookstore and fountain (the Coop) opened in the temporary buildings south of the main building. Technological gadgetry appeared on campus in the forms of a dictaphone in the president's office, and a Frigidaire and an oil burner range in the college commons kitchen!

Not-So-New Deal Students

Mock presidential elections in 1932 and 1936 indicated the student body at Humboldt, contrary to national trends, was largely conservative. Republicans Herbert Hoover and Alf Landon carried the campus electorate. At one point in 1939 a campus controversy emerged over whether even to allow classroom discussion of Franklin D. Roosevelt's New Deal!

The world was discussing strategies for world peace, the effectiveness of the League of Nations in restraining the Japanese in Manchuria and China, responses to the Italian invasion of Ethiopia, and the rise of Adolph Hitler in Germany. Mounting war clouds gave pertinence to Congressional Nye Committee hearings, which charged undue influence by munitions makers in causing war.

Humboldt students, however, showed more interest in campus life than in military campaigns. If *Lumberjack* editorials and articles are a good measure, prime issues of concern included women smoking, inadequate school spirit, the best method of hitchhiking between Eureka and Arcata, and the price of a milk shake (12 cents) at the college commons. As for issues of aggression — an unusually heavy snowfall in January, 1932, prompted snowball fights. The result of this local aggression: four broken windows.

Social activities tended toward the traditional: the Masked Ball, the Junior Prom, the Senior Banquet and Ball. An All-

College Picnic graced each spring. The Associated Students budget for 1933-34 totaled $4,368. Of that amount, dramatics received $1,092 and athletics $1,120. By the end of the decade, several new organizations supplemented existing club life, including a Forestry Club (1938) and a revitalized Associated Women Students (1939). To increase the coverage of campus and community activities, as well as to promote advertising, *The Lumberjack* changed from a biweekly to a weekly paper in the fall of 1936.

Student government broadened in the 30s, especially the board of control, which sought to monitor student behavior. The board reprimanded students for making "general whoopee" in the library, for unauthorized borrowing from lockers, and for stealing the California Bear flag from the auditorium. In 1933 they took away a block H (varsity letter) from a football player seen in the early morning hours of game day "in a public dance pavilion in Eureka."

Athletics

Sports represented the major extracurricular activity during these years. Much of this was men's and women's intramural competition, including archery, golf, and volleyball. The Women's Athletic Association continued to sponsor Play Day.

Intercollegiate tennis and track teams competed for the first time in the mid-30s. The Humboldt men played basketball against Civilian Conservation Corps workers from Prairie Creek and Orleans.

There was talk of dropping football because of the expense and the lack of a proper field. In a 1933 election, students voted 116-74 to keep it. College teams to the south, however, did not like playing here because of travel and weather — the same complaints heard today — so Humboldt played mostly local high schools. A 20-member football team sported a 6-1-6 record in 1935, a good beginning for the school's first winning football coach, Charles Erb.

Fred Telonicher described Erb as "a master at firing a team up prior to each game." Erb coached the Humboldt Thun-

derbolts to three winning seasons, highlighted by a 1936 victory over San Jose State, 20-0. Earl Meneweather, Frank Simas, Vernon Thornton, Len Longholm, and Franny Moore starred on these early teams. In 1939 students changed the team's nickname to Lumberjacks.

Community Relations

North Coast transportation stood much improved from the school's earliest years. Humboldt grads Eugene Fountain and Paul Hunter drove from Berkeley to Arcata in only 14 hours in 1938. Still, 14 hours! The area's isolation may, however, have contributed to better college/community relations.

Most students were locals, of course. Nearly all alumni association activities involved former students originally from the local community, including presidents Lena Moll Gilmore, Alta McElwain Monroe, Clyde Patenaude, Ethel Pedrassini Scott, Les Stromberg, and Walter Schocker. The *Humboldt Alumnus,* first published in 1934, chronicled the strong ties developing between town and gown.

Of particular note was the local support in building a badly needed dormitory. In her history of Humboldt State College, written in 1947, Sarah Davies recounted a troubling visit by Assemblyman Michael Burns in 1937. Having inspected Sunset Hall, HSC's only dormitory, he wrote:

> The approach to San Quentin prison is impressive and well kept; the approach to the student dormitory at Humboldt State College is ugly and depressing.

He spoke of worn-off paint, foundation problems, missing shingles from the roof, windows stuffed with newspapers to keep out wind and rain, and the lack of hot water. He noted that students had to walk through wind and rain to use the two toilets, one for men and one for women. With the help of community appeals to Sacramento, the state legislature appropriated funds for a new dormitory (Nelson Hall) in 1939.

(*clockwise*) The new gymnasium, 1933; Plant Operations personnel, 30s; athletic field on the site of Redwood Bowl.

Scenes from the College Elementary School: (*clockwise from top right*) east view of Gist Hall in the 30s; close-up of exterior east wall mural; student reenactment of the *Laura Virginia* discovering Humboldt Bay; slide beside the south stairs.

42

Humboldt State's relations with the business community were good. Local merchants enjoyed economic benefits from the student population and gladly advertised in *The Lumberjack*. (Daly's, for example, advertised $2.95 corduroy skirts in 1935.) The community also patronized the college plays, musicals, and dramas, thus contributing monies to the student loan fund.

The campus reciprocated. Even in the worst Depression times, not all the school's attention focused inward. Dramas at the Minor Theatre raised money for a community unemployment relief fund. Special courses and lectures helped explain to the public the various provisions of the Social Security Act, the National Recovery Act, and the National Labor Relations Act.

A Student-Centered Institution

The 1935 name change from Humboldt State Teachers College to Humboldt State College acknowledged the changing nature of the school's academic programs. The training of teachers remained primary, but now several nonteaching and preprofessional programs existed as well.

The lower division liberal arts program (junior college component) and a two-year commerce course continued, as did pre-professional programs in agriculture, forestry, nursing, and engineering. Humboldt also offered pre-secondary teaching programs in applied arts, biology, English, and social science. In 1937 HSC was authorized to offer a B.S. degree in education. Thereafter the school added liberal arts degree programs in economic and business administration, speech, and home economics.

President Gist established a chart of duties to promote administrative efficiency. He appointed Homer Balabanis as vice president and director of summer session. Gist gave professional rank to each instructor and began the rotation of department chairs. He also encouraged faculty to earn the Ph.D. and engage in professional growth activities.

"Baly"

Since Homer Balabanis advised the student government and taught Econ 1, a required freshman course, he knew nearly every student. One year Baly gave his class a test just before Christmas vacation. One student read through the test questions, decided he wasn't quite up to answering them, and in the spirit of the season wrote on the bottom of the test: "Only God knows the answers to these questions. Merry Christmas." After the holidays, when the student got back his test paper, he found this message from Baly: "God gets an A. You get an F. Happy New Year."

National and world events may have proved depressing, but morale didn't suffer much at Humboldt. On the eve of World War II, a burgeoning liberal arts curriculum boosted spirits. The College Elementary School was producing both well-educated children and student teachers with considerable teaching experience under competent supervisors. Homer Balabanis would later write:

> The small faculty and enrollment permitted close personal relations between faculty and students and among faculty and administrators. What we could not offer in material goods, we tried to offer in human values. The institution was student centered, and the faculty had a stake in the survival and reputation of the institution. Personal advantage was minimized and a high quality of instruction was maintained.

(*clockwise from top right*) Fred Telonicher, assistant football coach, 1938; Charles Fulkerson, professor of music; Coach Charley Erb; Sunset Hall, built from part of the old "temporary" buildings.

44

(*clockwise from top left*) Coeds of the 30s initiating a freshman in the courtyard fountain, and relaxing in front of the cafeteria; 1937 football stars(*l-r*) Earl Meneweather, Franny Moore, Toy Ferin, and Wendel"Windy" Moore.

45

**Spring
Fever**

Everyone needs a vacation come springtime, even if that vacation is called Work Day. Freed from classroom responsibilities for a day, Humboldt students and faculty would clean up and improve the campus. But "work" hardly describes the atmosphere.

Part of the annual tradition was an 8 a.m. Faculty Show designed "to pep up the student body and to inspire them to superhuman work on their jobs." The students loved it. Some years, two shows were scheduled to accommodate the crowds. Performances included a mock opera, a minstrel show, a male-faculty hula dance, and an annual solo sung by Homer Balabanis. In yet another performance, a bathing profes-

sor, Ed Jeffers, was pulled across stage in a big wash tub.

Following the show, students and faculty rolled up their sleeves and got to work. The project might be building a trail to Council Crest or washing windows or replanting gardens. One year they built a barbecue as a memorial for students fighting in World War II. In 1947 the school called two consecutive Work Days in order to construct

the east stands of Redwood Bowl.

Unfortunately, when enrollment expanded into the thousands, students just didn't know all the faculty. The Faculty Show lost its punch and was discontinued. The demise of Work Day soon followed. But for decades to come, the campus still found time each spring for All-College Picnics, Lumberjack Days, and salmon bakes at Camp Bauer.

The War Years

1939 - 46

"... then the whole world got screwed up ..."

Hitler's blitzkrieg through Poland in September, 1939, officially launched World War II. Congress passed the Selective Service Act in September, 1940. On December 7, 1941, the Japanese bombed Pearl Harbor, drawing the U.S. into the war.

As on so many other campuses, the war effort dramatically affected students and faculty. Franny Givins, 1940 graduate, spoke for many when he said, "We were always dreaming about doing something great. And then the whole world got screwed up, so a lot of those things didn't happen."

Between national mobilization for the war effort, rationing, the recruiting and drafting of students and faculty, campus camouflaging, blackouts and air raid drills, evacuation plans, USO dances with the sailors, and letter writing campaigns to boost the spirits of service persons — *everybody* in one way or another felt the effects of the war. A student couldn't *just* think about education. For many of those left behind, the war effort helped promote a strong sense of community.

The Girls' Seminary

Enrollment varied considerably during the war years: from 436 in 1939, to a low of 159 in the spring of 1945. Nearly all came from Humboldt County or the North Coast.

Men temporarily outnumbered women 203-197 in the fall of 1940. This would reverse dramatically as the U.S. became involved in the war. Of 27 graduates in 1944, only four were men. At one point in 1945, only one male student remained on campus. Faith Adams Dikas, 1945 graduate, remembered HSC being referred to as a "girls' seminary."

HSC campus, post-World War II.

Work on the new dormitory, Nelson Hall, began in 1939. The name honored Hans Nelson, state senator, partly responsible for the founding of Humboldt State and a supporter throughout the years. Completed in 1940, Nelson Hall provided an infirmary, a dining hall, a reception room, a lounge, and 76 bed spaces, two students to a room. Planners intended one wing for men and one for women, but during World War II women occupied most of both wings.

Monica Hadley, dean of women in 1938, recalled that the women did not want to make their own rules. "They would rather have someone else make the rules so they could break them and have all this fun."

The faculty and administration expected future teachers — and women in particular — to conduct themselves in a manner reflecting well on Humboldt. In 1940 Hadley chastised her coeds for chewing gum in public:

> Previously those Humboldt women who chewed gum were the exception, but today it seems to be the rule, particularly with the freshmen.

47

(*clockwise from top right*) Dean of Women, Monica Hadley, 1940; soda fountain in the student Coop; library in Founders Hall; Nelson Hall.

But campus life for women consisted of more than study and rigid discipline. During the war years, Hadley herself took HSC women to the Naval Air Station in McKinleyville to dance with the sailors stationed there.

The Wartime Campus

Even before Pearl Harbor, the tone on campus had become much more serious. The previous decade's debates over school spirit and milk shake prices had given way to student and faculty forums on whether women should have careers after marriage or whether the U.S. should declare war on the Axis. After Pearl Harbor, public debate turned to women's role in the war effort, the post-war shift in education bound to occur, and voting and educational opportunities after the war for Japanese-Americans, African-Americans, and other minorities.

Before Pearl Harbor, the Mutsuhito Club had sponsored the campus queen selection and generally promoted school spirit. After December 7, 1941, however, the club changed its name to Favonians to eliminate connections with anything Japanese.

The entire campus mobilized for the war effort. An air observation post, atop Pop Jenkins' industrial arts shop south of the main building, employed the eyes and ears of faculty and their spouses. Campus leaders conducted blackouts and air raid drills.

The Lumberjack initiated a column, "With the Armed Forces," to relate news of service persons. *Humboldt Hilarities,* a campus variety show, presented "The War Effort" in 1942 to rouse spirits. In 1944 patriots set up a stamp shack in front of the main building to sell war bonds and stamps for the specific purpose of purchasing an army jeep ($1,165).

Still, a semblance of normality endured. Students danced away their noon hours in the gym. Alta Fulton, Mary Acheson, and Gilly Negro reigned as campus queens in the early 40s. The Steamboat Shuffle had students dancing on the decks of the *Antelope,* a steam ferry on Humboldt Bay. Long Conga lines formed at the yearly Sadie Hawkins hop.

Fees varied little during the war: $25-26 per year, including yearbook, health, and hospitalization fees.

Freshmen got doused in the "fish pond" in the courtyard of the administration building. The Frosh-Soph Brawl maintained its roughhouse tradition. (Freshmen would build an eminently combustible structure, then try to keep the sophomores from burning it down.) Pop Jenkins sponsored bean feeds, taffy pulls, and Camp Bauer pancake feeds. He also made doughnuts for everyone in his big iron pot.

Associated Men and Women Students, Forestry Club, Women's Athletic Association, and College "Y" continued. The HSC choir and ASB officers made goodwill tours of the North Coast to recruit students. *Humboldt Hilarities* continued until director Don Karshner went to war with the seabees in 1943. (This popular tradition resumed upon his return.) Work Day lasted until 1943, when it was abandoned for the duration of the war.

Athletics

Men's intercollegiate sports achieved a modicum of success just before the war's intervention. In 1940 the college affiliated with the Far Western Conference. HSC began competing in football that fall but then abolished it "for the duration" in 1942.

Coach Earl Hoos suggested replacing the sport with a Commando Physical Fitness Program to prepare Humboldt men for military service. Baseball coach Marty Mathiesen directed the program, which included an obstacle run across Mad River during the rainy season.

Men's basketball competition was limited mostly to games with military service teams from Orick, Eureka, and McKinleyville. These teams formed a Hoop League in 1943 with the stipulation, "wins and losses will not count, and [we] will not play for a trophy."

Athletic stars in this era included Bill Farber, Leo Sullivan, Frank Simas, Butch Caviness, Fritz Littlejohn, Frank Sanderson, Harry Wineroth, Toy Ferin, Franny Moore, Earl

Remembering the War Effort

"In 1942-43, at the start of the war," Don Karshner recalled, "Charlie Fulkerson and I shared a National Defense skywatch in a privy-like addition on top of Pop Jenkins' old shop from 2 to 6 a.m. every week. The wind howled and the rain poured, so we rarely heard an airplane fly over Arcata."

Observers who did hear an airplane reported immediately to National Defense headquarters in San Francisco. Gayle Karshner recalls, "Faculty wives served at the listening post. On a foggy day we often heard logging trucks in low gear grinding up the G Street hill, which was Highway 101 through Arcata then, and we mistakenly called San Francisco, because the sound was similar to that of an airplane. Defense officials were probably amazed at the amount of air activity over Arcata."

In the afternoons, women got together to knit — either socks for servicemen or "baby soakers." (Since civilians could obtain no rubber or plastic, wetting babies wore wool panties called "soakers.")

Meat and gasoline were rationed, blackouts were enforced, and the highway speed limit was reduced to 35 m.p.h. Women saved kitchen fats for use in making munitions. In the drive to collect scrap metals, there was a movement to turn in the Arcata Plaza statue of President McKinley to be melted down for arms.

HSC classes often were disrupted by the deafening roar and vibration of a blimp hovering low over the court of Founders Hall — mainly to impress the college girls who attended parties at the blimp base on the Samoa Peninsula.

Barn Dance

recalled by
Gayle Karshner

At each year's fall Barn Dance, the tiny old gymnasium below the president's house was decorated with bales of hay, cornstalks, pumpkins, farm wagons, buckboards, harrows, and the like. For the 1941 Barn Dance, Howard Goodwin, Leonard Longholm and possibly Maury Ayala or Harvey del Fatti, liberated a classic two-holer privy from a farm on Dow's Prairie. Though the privy was the star attraction at the dance, the theft did not go unchallenged. That privy had been in current operation, and the farmer was understandably irate over its unauthorized removal. Many had witnessed the strange cargo in its transport south on Highway 101, and the farmer soon tracked his possession to the gym. President Gist made the culprits repair and reinstall the Barn Dance attraction.

Meneweather, and Wendel "Windy" Moore in football; Franny Givins, Billy Lee, Vernon Thornton, Lee Seidell, and Ken Brantley in basketball.

HSC women participated in only one intercollegiate event during the war, a Women's Western Intercollegiate Archery Tournament in 1944. Contestants mailed their results to Los Angeles. Humboldt placed fourth of 24 colleges, and Anna Babler tied for second individual honors.

Skiing became a popular new intramural sport. A ski club built Lumberjack Ski Lodge on Horse Mountain in 1939.

Allies in the Community

Friendliness and a cooperative spirit between college and community continued during the war years. Arcata's city defense council, for instance, included HSC in their evacuation plans in 1942. Theirs, too, was the suggestion to camouflage the main building (Founders Hall). Local citizens feared its becoming a target for offshore Japanese subs. The council made its request in 1942, but the state did not provide funds for the painting until the spring of 1944, long after any real danger existed. Fishing boats soon replaced submarines (real or imagined) in the bay, yet those walls remained a bilious, camouflage green until 1948.

The HSC Improvement Association continued its strong support in these years. Local service organizations, in turn, borrowed campus facilities for their discussions and fundraisers. One of these public events, Pan American Day, promoted better relations and defense solidarity among the Americas.

Academic Affairs

At the behest of professors William and Hortense Lanphere, Humboldt began a wildlife management program in 1940, reportedly the first such program in California. Facilities included a hatchery (for instructive purposes) and game-rearing pens. Students could sign up for "Conservation of Wildlife," or take "Game Bird Management," a far cry from the destructive events half a world away.

Humboldt's Ski Club

Dr. Bob Bryan ('42), second president of Humboldt's Ski Club, believes the local winter climate was colder and wetter in the pre-war days. A minor climatic shift occurred about that time.

The Ski Club had as many as 60 members, several of whom actually knew how to ski. Marianne Lambert Pinches ('42, an officer of the club who never skied) remembers that it was all great fun. Their February snow carnival was praised in the 1940 *Sempervirens* as "a tumbling success."

The club built its lodge in 1939 according to plans drawn up by sponsor William Lanphere. The cabin site was three miles in on Titlow Hill Road. Bob Bryan and some friends were at the ski lodge in 1941 when they got the disturbing news of Pearl Harbor. Several months later, Bryan and his wife honeymooned in that same cabin. (In those days, gas rationing made it difficult — and unpatriotic — to go off some place more exotic.) The lodge was later rented out to loggers who, while cutting a tree for firewood, lost control of the tree. It rolled downhill into the cabin and shook it off its foundation. Eventually the lodge was burned down.

51

But the war dictated many of the curricular changes of this era. HSC offered aeronautic meteorology, navigation, wartime conversational French, Navy V-1 and V-5 programs, and "The War Today." For women, the school offered radio training, knitting, and sewing.

Although the total number of faculty and staff did not change significantly during the war, many took leave to serve the nation in military or civilian capacities.

Vice president Homer Balabanis served with the Office of Price Administration and with the state department in Washington, D.C.; professor of education Harry Griffith served in the air force in Salinas; drama instructor John Van Duzer spent a semester in the army, and his colleague Don Karshner served in the seabees; accounting officer Gene Flocchini was stationed in Texas; biology professor Harry MacGinitie was stationed in New Mexico; and the president's secretary, Sarah Davies, worked for Pan American Airlines.

Several faculty wives filled in as instructors. Hazel Jeffers took over her husband Edmund's music classes. Charles Fulkerson was joined by his wife Jean, an excellent cellist. Following the war, she continued teaching string classes for many years. Gayle Karshner taught speech and drama for her husband Don and for John Van Duzer. She also directed all the plays. Men were scarce among the students, so faculty were recruited for male roles. All-women casts were common. Nell Murphy took her husband George's position in the English department.

The Northwest Association of Secondary and Higher Schools granted accreditation to Humboldt State in 1944. But a shortage of library facilities and low enrollment kept a secondary school credential program from being offered.

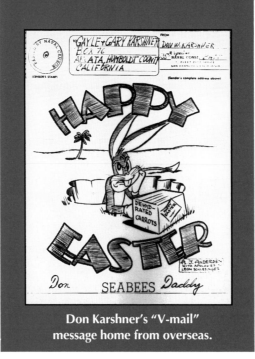

Don Karshner's "V-mail" message home from overseas.

Letters to (and from) the Troops

Perhaps the most successful and comprehensive effort to mobilize the campus was President Gist's crusade to encourage letters and commendations for former Humboldters serving in the armed forces.

The responding letters from the soldiers indicate the success of the campaign. In 1945 Willard Woodcock reported from New Guinea that he had received "three boxes and 28 letters during the mail rush!" According to James Roscoe, Gist wrote personally to virtually every Humboldt service person. By late 1943 Gist had worked up a list of 275 names and addresses.

From Christmas of 1943 until Christmas of 1945 the *Humboldt News Letter* delivered news from home to all known military personnel (from the Gist list) who had attended Humboldt State. An editorial staff of Claire Speier Gustafson, Edward Graves, Maurice Hicklin, Emmalena Thomson, Jessie Woodcock, Sarah Davies, and William McMillan put out the four-page newsletter. It contained news of the college, news of service persons' activities, and excerpts from letters. The *News Letter* undoubtedly provided good cheer to those in the war. The close-knit camaraderie of Humboldt State was thus exported to all parts of the world.

Correspondents included Stanley Roscoe (army air force), Donald Falk and Wesley Graham (army), Gene Orlandi (artillery), Herb Gomes and Walter Schocker (marines), Leno Canclini (navy), and hundreds of others. Bob Oliveira found himself stationed in Hawaii, Reno Orlandi, Italy; Robert Bonner, Saipan; Ledo Matteoli, China; Joe Rezzonico, Australia; Paul Hunter, Iran; and Alan Lufkin, the Dutch East Indies.

(clockwise from top right)) House moving, a common sight on the 40s campus; Ed Jeffers, assistant professor of music, scrubbing his way through the 1941 Faculty Show; 1944 production of *Junior Miss* with *(l-r)* Professor William Lanphere, students Jean Hardwick, Ellen Peterson, and Professor Charles Fulkerson.

Former football coach Charlie Erb held the rank of major, working with combat intelligence in the South Pacific. Football star-turned-sergeant Earl Meneweather wrote from Germany in 1945 that he'd gladly settle for one small piece of land under the north goal post on Humboldt's old practice field. Mike Chetkovich served as chief engineer on a ship in the Pacific. Charles Waters sent a Nazi flag to President Gist as a war souvenir from Germany. And at least two heroic Humboldters received the Bronze Star: William Nellist and Joe Walsh.

Humboldt women involved in the war effort included Christine Jacobsen and June Mair (SPARs); Faith Hope and Georgia Williams (navy nurses); Rae Bengston (army); Betty Hess Carter, Marilyn Colney, Dorothy Dillon, and Betty Jean Abbott (WAVEs); Joyce Abbott (WAACs); and Thais Baldwin (navy). Clarice Johnson, an army nurse in the North African and Italian campaigns, wrote from Anzio in 1944: "When the bombing started, a foxhole was appreciated more than a room in the Palace Hotel."

One of the newsletter's unstated purposes was to entice military personnel to return to Humboldt and complete their degrees. Articles mentioned the "six units of block credit" for military service and gave updates on pending congressional legislation to provide educational benefits for veterans (the Servicemen's Readjustment Act of 1944, more commonly referred to as the G.I. Bill).

Many did return to Humboldt. They constituted the early and significant increase in enrollment in the late 40s following the end of the war.

Preparing for Peace

After the defeat of Germany and Japan in 1945, the campus, with the rest of the nation, began its difficult conversion to peacetime.

A constant teacher shortage had existed during the war. In 1944 HSC reported a 97 percent placement rate for its new teachers. This fact encouraged optimism on campus, as did the new G.I. Bill and prospects for soon offering a B.A. in secondary education.

Throughout 1945-46 HSC prepared for the influx of students. Repairs and physical improvements were made on campus and a new football coach, Joseph Forbes, was hired so the sport could resume in the fall of 1946.

HSC implemented a new academic organization in the spring of 1946. Curricular offerings fell into two main categories under the leadership of two academic deans: the dean of education and the dean of arts and sciences.

> Dean of Education
> > Education courses
> > Teacher-education program
>
> Dean of Arts & Sciences
> > Fine & Applied Arts
> > Health & Physical Education
> > Language & Literature
> > Natural Sciences
> > Social Sciences

To close out the story of the war: by one report, 585 men who had attended HSC had served in the military. Eighteen were known dead, and five were missing.

HSC faculty and staff, 1946: 1- Kenneth Bailey 2- Roy Bohler 3- Bert Wilson 4- "Pop" Jenkins 5- Arthur Gist 6- William Lanphere 7- Helen Everett 8- Imogene Platt 9- Richard Meade 10- Maurice Hicklin 11- Michael Chetkovitch 12- Harry MacGinitie 13- John Van Duzer 14- Belle Dickson 15- Elizabeth Brizard 16- Homer Balabanis 17- George Murphy 18- Adella Johnson 19- Myrtle McKittrick 20- Don Karshner 21- Eugene Flocchini 22- Dorothy Gentry 23- Frances Yocum 24- Hazel Jeffers 25- Stella Little 26- Eugenia Loder

Buffalo Heads

from the collected
speeches of
Don Karshner

In the 30s and 40s, when many colleges' professors still addressed one another formally—*Mister* or *Sir*, for example— Humboldt State maintained an air of informality and friendliness.

It knew its faculty as Pop (Jenkins), Mac (MacGinitie), Baly (Homer Balabanis), Major (Maurice Hicklin), Murf (George Murphy), Griff (Harry Griffith), and Charlie F. (Fulkerson). With twenty-some faculty and a total enrollment under 400, everyone knew everyone, and fast friendships were formed.

In the 50s many of these long-time friends formed a loose organization known as the Buffalo Heads. These were "the real Humboldters," those who had arrived before the dramatic growth and depersonalization of the 50s.

The Buffalo Heads could remember when most faculty lived in houses on campus. They could remember Fred Telonicher and his wife Margaret hatching pheasant eggs in their oven to help start the wildlife program. Or Charlie F. playing Bach piano sonatas in a college assembly by day and Boogie Woogie in a dance band by night. Or Major Hicklin walking his beautiful elkhound Holly about the campus. Or all of them sneaking with

the men students for an all-day spring beer bust down by the Van Duzen River. Or Bill Johnson — an institution as chief of maintenance— helping hundreds of students with part-time jobs, helping the faculty with their office and household repairs, and taking the lead in the construction of Redwood Bowl.

But times changed. Bob Gayhart's Varsity Sweet Shop in Arcata was no longer the student hangout. California Barrel was no longer the big employer in Arcata. And the college itself became so large that faculty members could pass their colleagues on the sidewalk and not even know their names. One by one the Buffalo Heads went out to pasture.

The HSC faculty in 1946.

55

56

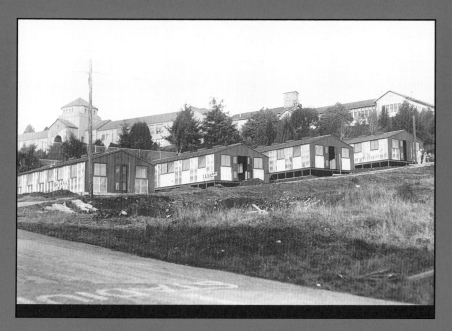

(clockwise from top right) Botany lab in basement of Founders Hall, 1939; William and Hortense Lanphere , professors of biology, 1940 (with their dog, "Hec"); temporary classrooms, 1946.

57

Humboldt Hilarities

In the 40s (with the exception of a couple of the war years), Humboldt Hilarities gave students a chance to show off their talents — or just show off. From 150 to 250 students (half, or more, of the student population) participated in the production of farces, satires, musical numbers, and dramatic pieces.

The 1947 theme parodied *Life* magazine with "articles" such as "*Life* Photographers Lost in Wilds of Northern California," "Report on Occupational Forces" (in Geisha houses), "Winter Sports at Ski Lodge," and "Over the Air Waves Cometh Tripe." The 1948 theme of "Past, Paste, & Posterity" was a cavalcade of college life

from Puritan days to the future era of rockets and atomic energy. Don Karshner, John Van Duzer, and Ted DeLay managed the productions. Don Karshner recalled dazzling patriotic finishes in the war years and more sophisticated songs and scripts after the older, returning GI's began handling the shows.

The finale — 1943 Humboldt Hilarities.

Peacetime Invasion

1946 - 53

Postwar Explosion

Enrollment averaged 255 in 1945-46, but the fall semester of 1946 would see that number leap to an astonishing 650! Growth surged to 751 in 1949-50 before the Korean conflict began taking away World War II veterans and college-aged youths. Those early increases, however, presented great challenges to President Gist and his successor Cornelius Siemens.

The G.I. Bill prompted the influx of students, as did California's population growth and the accompanying demand for more teachers. In 1948 the state department of education predicted Humboldt's student population would reach 1575 by 1965. In fact, it reached twice that number before 1960.

Much of the close-knit camaraderie, informality, and friendliness so characteristic of HSC since its founding would be lost in the growth. In purely physical terms, increased enrollment would precipitate a critical housing and classroom shortage.

Kenneth Bailey, dean of students, arranged for a barracks near the site of today's wildlife building. The barracks (named Redwood Hall) housed men. Nelson Hall, then, became exclusively a women's dorm in 1947. JoAnne Wilson Dale related that women residents grew plants in the urinals of what was formerly the men's bathrooms. HSC also built thirty housing units for married students just southwest of College Elementary School. Named Humboldt Village, locals dubbed it G.I. Village because of the many veterans living there.

Humboldt Village, 1949.

In a complete turnabout from the first half of the decade, men now clearly outnumbered women — three to one in 1946. North Coast residents still made up the majority, but the percentage of students from San Francisco and the bay area increased steadily.

Especially after Siemens became president, the college looked abroad for new students. By 1952 HSC had small contingents from the Near East, Germany, Yugoslavia, and the U.S. territories of Samoa, Guam, and Hawaii.

Enrollment fell again during the Korean War (624 in 1950-51; 592 in 1951-52; 563 in 1952-53). A Greater Humboldt Committee of faculty and students recruited actively in high schools across Northern California. In 1951 the committee reinstituted Senior Days on campus.

New Faces

The faculty jumped from 27 to 63 full-time instructors. New and soon to be familiar faces on campus included Leland Barlow (music); Kate Buchanan and John Pauley (speech/drama); Reese Bullen (art); Joseph Forbes, Louise Watson, and Ced Kinzer (physical education); William Jackson (business); Hyman Palais (history); Roscoe Peithman (physics); Daniel Brant (biology); Charles Bloom (librarian); Kathryn Corbett (sociology); Lawrence Marx (psychology); Giles Sinclair (English); Frank Wood (foreign language); William Raleigh (education); Edwin Pierson (forestry); and Mark B. Rhea (agriculture).

In 1947 a beginning assistant professor with a master's degree earned $3,540 per year. (Forty years later, the same assistant professor, with a doctorate, would earn $27,000.)

The recruiting of faculty sometimes surprised the recruited. Joseph Forbes, like so many, pictured HSC just a short distance north of San Francisco. He and his family drove up from Los Angeles during the 1945 Christmas holidays.

> After a leisurely trip north with my family, we suddenly found ourselves stranded in Willits during a monsoon, with water several feet over Highway 101. We finally arrived days later . . . A tour of the campus (it took ten minutes in those days) revealed that the stadium was only partially completed, with no bleachers and no sign of turf. The track was a mass of sub-surfacing boulders, and the only structure for physical education was a leaky little gym.

Forbes had an alternative offer in San Diego and was "firmly resolved to flee." But warm student and community support, the wonderful physical surroundings, and "the charm of Homer Balabanis and his tales of the potentials" persuaded Forbes to take the position.

Balabanis wrote, "What we could not offer in material goods, we tried to offer in human values."

Academic & Administrative Changes

By 1947 HSC was authorized to offer a credential in secondary teaching, thus making it a five-year institution. The first graduate courses, in history, met that fall.

A new B.A. in wildlife management; a speech/radio major; a M.A. in the teaching of drama, education, and social sciences; two-year programs in forestry/lumbering and dairying/agriculture — all these changed the face of the Humboldt State College curriculum. By 1953 HSC offered nearly 30 baccalaureate degrees and was featuring the natural resource areas more and more.

Significant reorganization came under President Gist in 1947. Three deans and the head librarian reported to the

president. The dean of the school of education, Ivan Milhous, oversaw teacher training and credential programs, aided by Harry Griffith (elementary education) and Albert Graves (secondary education).

The dean of the school of arts and sciences, Homer Balabanis, administered five divisions:

> Fine & Applied Arts
> > Don Karshner, division head
> Health & Physical Education
> > Harold Bishop, division head
> Language & Literature
> > Maurice Hicklin, division head
> Natural Sciences
> > Harry MacGinitie, division head
> Social Science
> > Kenneth Bailey, division head

Eugenia Loder, dean of women: George Murphy, dean of men; and Helen Everett, librarian, looked after students outside the classroom.

The following year, after pressure by Helen Everett and the Association of California State College Instructors, Gist appointed an advisory council — still in existence — composed of deans, division heads, the registrar, librarian, and other faculty and staff. This body advised the president on college policies.

End of the Gist Era

President Gist suffered a heart attack in November, 1949, and retired the following June.

Arthur Gist had served 20 years as president — through the Depression, war, and postwar reconversion. When he arrived, Humboldt had three credential programs, 27 faculty, and 372 students. When he left two decades later, HSC had 31 degree programs, 47 faculty, and 751 students. Gist had taken pride in fostering a closeness with students and faculty. He also cultivated the relationship between campus and the community. However, as Balabanis noted,

When the college grew, problems became more complicated and relations became less personal. The president saw his ideal vanishing. His ideal was "our small, friendly college." Especially after 1946, the college was neither small nor as friendly.

He was perturbed particularly by the growth of the liberal arts program and at its faculty which, he feared, undermined the main function of Humboldt State College: that is, teacher education — his main interest.

Cornelius Siemens Arrives

During Gist's illness, interim president Homer Balabanis drew up Humboldt's first master plan (a process now mandated by the state). The plan called for a half-billion dollar budget and eleven major construction projects, including a fine and applied arts building (with auditorium), a student activities building (with cafeteria), a swimming pool and gymnasium, a metal shop, an administration building, and buildings for wildlife, science, and health science.

After Gist announced his retirement, a search committee hired Cornelius Siemens as his successor. Russian-born Siemens had earned his Ph.D. from the University of California, Berkeley. He had taught mathematics at San Diego State and served as president of Compton College.

Siemens took office on July 1, 1950, and immediately launched a vigorous campaign to fulfill the master plan aspirations of 1949. He left curricular developments largely to Balabanis, and chose to devote his time to physical development of the campus, finances, and public relations. In October, 1950, he announced an ambitious program of construction: 14 new buildings.

He also appointed an HSC advisory board of community members headed by Don O'Kane, Humboldt County

President Cornelius Siemens

newspaper publisher. Later, that board would perform perhaps its most significant action: lobbying the governor to veto legislation condemning HSC to "grade B" status for salary and funding purposes. Humboldt maintained full parity with other state schools.

In 1951 President Siemens reorganized and expanded administrative lines of authority as mandated by the state. The president was advised by his own council, Executive Dean Lawrence Turner, the advisory board, and the HSC Improvement Association. Jessie Woodcock served as business manager. Homer Balabanis, now dean of instruction, oversaw seven academic divisions. The division of education and psychology, lead by Ivan Milhous, housed the teacher training program. Dean of Students Leonard Christensen ministered to student needs and activities. Edward Girard would be appointed associate dean of students (guidance) in 1952.

Siemens also established the HSC Foundation to promote and fund the educational and research goals of the college.

Campus Construction

With the postwar surge in enrollment, the campus experienced dramatic physical change. Six prefabricated buildings south of the tennis courts became classrooms. A Quonset hut east of the gym handled extra physical education classes. Varsity Hall, erected as a temporary dormitory for varsity athletes, was remodeled in 1950 to become the new Coop (soda fountain, bookstore, and student offices).

In 1950, California's department of public works issued a report that nearly all of Humboldt's buildings needed "urgent" or "necessary" repair, and *every* building needed painting. A surge of construction in the 50s and 60s would remedy those problems.

The developing
50s campus:
(clockwise) **The
Coop and Nelson
Hall across a
crowded parking
lot; the Quonset
hut gymnasium;
excavation for
the new library
on the south end
of Founders Hall;
Jenkins Hall un-.
der construction.**

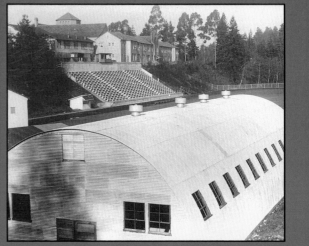

(*clockwise from top right*) Students take a coffee break at the Coop, 1951; business students hard at work; the campus bookstore.

Remembering the Siemens

Sources: reminiscences of Gayle Karshner; Michael Corcoran, "Twenty Years in the Presidency," *Arcata Union,* April 9, 1970.

Upon his appointment at HSC, Cornelius Siemens ("Neil") became one of the youngest college presidents in the country. Yet he had already distinguished himself as writer and teacher. He had, for instance, authored a text on aeronautics and helped the Civil Aeronautics Administration set up its flight training program.

At Humboldt he immersed himself in both campus and community life, following interests ranging from baccalaureate degrees to Boy Scouts to Baptists. He also grew to be a well-known figure in the corridors of the state capitol, where he lobbied extensively for HSC and served on the California Constitution Revision Commission.

"There isn't a day or an hour," he said, "whether I'm on this campus or off it, that I don't totally identify myself with Humboldt. One builds a tremendous pride in this college. I feel hurt when someone criticizes it. I feel personally responsible for interpreting the college to people on the outside. I explain it, sell it, and brag about it."

His wife Olga, whom he met as a student at Berkeley, also involved herself on campus and in the community. An enthusiastic hostess, she personally planned menus, cooked, and decorated for social events in the president's home and on campus. Her gracious thank you notes and her prompt notes of appreciation to performers, achieving students, and faculty were prized. She sang in college music groups and did some solo work. In appreciation for her tireless interest and giving, students dedicated the 1958 issue of *Sempervirens* to her.

Siemens family: (*back*) Cornelius, Olga, (*front l-r*) Joan, "Belle", and Ronald. Another son, Mark, was born later.

Jenkins Hall, an industrial arts building completed in 1950, honored Pop Jenkins, who retired in 1953. In spring of 1953 the library, the biological sciences building (Science A today), and the corporation building opened their doors.

The library building, now Van Matré Hall, occupied only half the space of the original design because the state appropriated only half the necessary money. This explains why the front entrance opens to the southwest of the structure: builders anticipated another half of the building where faculty and staff park today.

Student Life

The late 40s saw a return to more traditional college activities. The influx of older students and several memorable incidents in these years would stretch the bounds of conventional campus activity. Most student life, however, tended toward the conservative and predictable.

Major issues for students ranged from parking violations (students were being called out of classes to remove illegally parked cars) to lack of school spirit; from housing shortages to students necking on the first date; from conservation of natural resources to certain instructors who insisted

A book burning took place on campus in the spring of 1953. Bobbysoxer co-eds and young men in rolled-up Levi's threw page after page onto the flames in front of the Coop. Actually, these students were only burning their textbooks to celebrate the end of final exams.

on punctuality for taking exams, then failed to return them on time! It was hardly a hotbed of radical social change.

Registration fees stayed between $25 and $32. Associated Student Body fees, however, increased considerably — as high as $25 by 1952. Many students refused to purchase ASB cards and support the nearly $40,000 ASB budget. An effort to make the cards mandatory failed in a campus election. This led the ASB to reduce prices at the Coop fountain in hopes of increasing their resources.

	ASB Cardholder	*Others*
Coffee	.07	.10
Milk Shake	.25	.35
Hamburger	.25	.30
Ham Sandwich	.30	.45
Potato Salad	.15	.35

The large numbers of veterans and married students might explain the lukewarm student participation in activities. The older students showed more interest in finishing degrees and moving on to jobs and "normal" lives.

The Lumberjack catered to this trend with its "Humboldt Village" and "Veteran's Corner" columns. Veterans' wives, mostly from Humboldt Village, formed a G.I. Wives Club. Information circulated about government assistance programs such as Cal-Vet and the G.I. Bill. Veterans received counseling, testing, special classes, and vocational guidance as the curriculum moved away from being exclusively teacher-training in orientation.

Though the career-minded veteran presence was not conducive to traditional school spirit, several new clubs did come into being in this era: Student Federalists (proponents of world government and peace), the Knights (promoting service and school spirit), the Wildlife Club, Conservation Unlimited (mostly wildlife and fisheries majors, involved in community conservation projects), a Newman Club, and Block H (varsity lettermen). A rally committee decorated for home sporting events, promoted attendance, and supported yell leaders and song queens. The campus hosted its first Harvest Ball and its first Sweetheart Ball in 1947.

A renewed emphasis on the fine arts led to two special events. The Northwestern California Drama Festival (for high school students) took place on campus in the fall of 1947. The following year HSC hosted its first major art festival. Art professors Reese Bullen and Melvin Schuler arranged for Bay Area artists to display their work.

Work Day was extended to two days in 1946 for the primary purpose of getting Redwood Bowl into shape for the football season. In later years Work Day linked a faculty variety show, a ravioli feed, and a dance with the usual efforts to spruce up the campus.

Homecoming was revitalized in 1946. Returning alumni joined the campus and community for a bean feed, bonfire, pep rally, hayride, parade, football game, and post-game dance.

The men's and women's student associations had been holding separate picnics. In 1949 both groups joined at Camp Bauer to revive the All-College Picnic.

The Conservation Week tradition began in 1950, coinciding with a greater emphasis on natural resources within the curriculum.

Whistling Pete

The postwar years seemed opportune for excessive nonsense and pranks. Joseph Forbes opined that many veterans had postponed a part of their childhood during the war. Their extracurricular activities plagued community and academe alike. They held beer-drinking sessions in Redwood Hall and put cows on the second floor of Nelson Hall. (Cows ascend stairs far more willingly than they descend.)

Chief among these pranks stands the infamous Whistling Pete caper. Whistling Pete was the cadaver used in biology and anatomy classes. One night a few students carted the corpse to Nelson Hall, the women's dormitory. Propping Pete against the front door, they rang the doorbell, and ran. Forbes said, "Screams could be heard all over Arcata."

Frances Ward Short tells of a less spectacular, but more common, way of living dangerously in those days: to cut classes and go to Clam Beach.

Just for the record, *Lumberjack* editorials denounced the aforementioned activities, characterizing them as "disgusting behavior."

Redwood Bowl & the Athletic Programs

As returning veterans swelled the ranks of men on campus, intercollegiate sports grew accordingly, especially football. Through the early months of 1946, students, faculty, and community members prepared Redwood Bowl for the football season. They built bleachers on both sides, covered the track with redwood bark, seeded the field, and built a press box and concession stand. Local lumber companies donated materials; local carpenters donated time.

The following year — thanks to a $4,000 loan taken out by President Gist, Joseph Forbes, and others — lights and a scoreboard made possible the first night games. Local merchants had been complaining about Saturday afternoon games detracting from business, and the state would not allow Sunday games.

HSC football boasted winning records between 1946-48. In 1952 coach Phil Sarboe led his Lumberjacks to their first Far Western Conference championship. An estimated 5,000 fans attended one game with UC Davis. Star players of these years — when helmets with face masks still were a rarity — included Gordon Schroeder, Tom Viracola, Tex McKown, Dick Lawitzke, Ray Mechals, Walt Greene, Jerry Garcia, Bob Dunaway, Jim McAuley, and Rudy Diaz.

The relatively successful 1946-47 basketball team featured all-American, Darrell Brown. The team fell on hard times, however, in subsequent years.

Track and field got up and running — stumbling, actually — with facilities that were marginal. Coach Joseph Forbes

(clockwise from top right) The Marching Lumberjacks of 1952; 1951 homecoming parade down G Street (then Highway 101); the Axe, fought over by Humboldt and Chico State in their football rivalry; an archery class takes aim.

67

reported, "The track had so many rocks in it that we immediately started hauling clay to cover the rocks." One star shone in those days: Claude Eshleman in the broad jump and high hurdles.

Women's athletics took place primarily on an intramural level under the sponsorship of the Women's Athletic Association.

Community Outreach

The joint effort to improve Redwood Bowl stands as just one of many examples of fine campus/community cooperation in this era. The HSC Improvement Association, the advisory board, and the HSC Foundation continued the tradition of partnership. Numerous community-sponsored scholarships evidenced a town-and-gown friendliness that thrived.

HSC reached out to local schools through music and dramatic festivals, the Women's Athletic Association's Play Day for high school girls, All-Star Day for local baseball enthusiasts, and the like. Jointly-sponsored musical offerings as diverse as opera and Bunny Hops took place in Eureka. Charles Fulkerson expanded the Humboldt Symphony which, by the 50s, numbered 60 musicians, including a strong community contingent.

The Red Scare

However, all was not harmony elsewhere in the world. Barely had the conversion to a peacetime environment commenced when the first hot war of the Cold War era exploded in Korea. Stateside, Senator Joseph McCarthy's witch hunts evidenced a new Red Scare.

McCarthyism had its impact on the HSC campus. A 1950 requirement compelled graduates to pass an examination in U.S. history and the constitution. *The Lumberjack* editorialized against compromising with communism in Korea. In 1952 Arcata police came on campus and arrested a man who identified himself as Mr. Fink of Santa Rosa, for distributing *People's World,* allegedly "a communist-inspired newspaper."

A 1950 *Lumberjack* faculty poll on the issue of loyalty oaths (by then required of all government employees in California) revealed, "The necessity of a livelihood is the stronger factor to the alternative of a feeble attempt to be a martyr."

As world events drew attention to the Far East and the Korean War, Humboldt students attending an all-college assembly discussed the issues of Nationalist versus Communist China, threats of another world war, the spread of communism, and "survival under atomic attack." A war memorial campaign promoted truth, peace, and justice. The campus conducted several blood donation drives. As in World War II, the college family participated in a letter-writing campaign to military service personnel.

Many students and faculty were recalled or drafted into military service. Education professor Ted Ingebritson, for example, was recalled to the Air Force. Potential draftees could, however, take the Selective Service college qualification test to earn a deferment. Many did. The Korean War affected enrollment considerably, but not as severely as World War II (the drop was from 751 to 653 students).

After 1953, enrollment would increase every year until 1975-76. This war, it seems, would only slow a process that had gathered considerable momentum since 1945.

(*clockwise from top right*) Leland Barlow leads caroling Sno-Ball Singers; library in what is now Van Matré Hall; art professors, Mel Schuler and Reese Bullen; calligraphy class; pottery class supervised by Pop Jenkins, 1952.

69

Memorable Pranks Throughout the Years

In the 40s, Imogene "Maddy" Platt was head resident of Sunset and Nelson Halls; and John Van Duzer, head resident of the men's wing of Nelson Hall. One Sunday morning, sleepy, conservative, easily scandalized Arcata awoke to find the marquee of the Arcata Theater announcing Maddy and John starring in the movie, *Twin Beds*.

In the 50s, a goat was found browsing on the flowers in the courtyard of the old administration building (Founders). A few years later, a burro browsed on that same spot. In 1954 a large Japanese artillery cannon from the front lawn of the Veterans Building (14th & J Streets) was found chained to the railing in front of Founders. No one seemed to know how it had gotten there. Two days later, just as mysteriously, it reappeared in its original place.

In the early 60s, several male residents of Redwood Hall held Moon Nights for the women in Sunset Hall. The women reciprocated with shows of their own, beginning to disrobe in front of their windows, then pulling the blinds at the crucial moment.

Meanwhile the Secret Comb Society placed the teeth of combs in all the locks to the new administration building (Siemens Hall). Later the society would claim credit for the placing of a Volkswagen in the hall in front of President Siemens' office, the moving of a faculty member's office furniture to the auditorium stage, and the publishing of a false *Daily Bulletin* reporting an all-college assembly at the same time and place as an actual CSC trustees meeting.

Members of the Secret Comb Society revealed themselves to Don Karshner, dean of students, just before their graduation. As he had suspected, the society's ranks included some of Humboldt's top student leaders.

Changing Times: Korea through Kennedy

1953 - 63

"The times they are a-changin'"

Following the Korean War, Humboldt State would experience well over two decades of consistent growth. That growth would not come without a certain amount of resistance, however. Local residents, for decades isolated by the topography, resented the sudden influx of outsiders. And the campus itself, like all of America, felt the tensions of the Cold War and the budding civil rights movement.

These were days of "I Like Ike," of President Kennedy's New Frontier, of McCarthyite suspicions, of atomic fallout shelters underneath American homes. Civil rights acts of 1957 and 1960 challenged long-held racist and segregationist attitudes. Humboldt State College struggled with all that, as well as with social problems all its own: the interpersonal strains and conflicts resulting from unprecedented growth.

Unveiling of the 1953 campus master plan. *(l-r)* Homer Balabanis, Helen Everett, J. Burton Vasche, President Siemens, Monroe Spaght, Mildred Turner, and Lawrence Turner.

On the one hand, President Cornelius Siemens lobbied Sacramento for exciting new campus construction projects to accommodate the ever-swelling ranks of students. On the other hand, Humboldt made concerted efforts to retain a sense of community and keep its reputation for small-campus friendliness. Already the school showed signs of weakening in that area. Segregation questions and Cold War issues would divide the campus community even further.

The Numbers

The student population increased to 812 in 1953-54. In the fall of 1954, Don Davis was recognized as the 1,000th student to enroll. By 1960 the student body surpassed 2,000.

Increased enrollment was attributed, in part, to the continuing effects of war. A few World War II veterans still attended. Korean veterans made up much of the late 50s influx. The Soviet Union's 1957 launching of Sputnik, a highly successful orbiting space satellite, created national insecurity. Fears that America's higher education was falling behind led the Cold War government to contribute generously to veterans through the National Defense Education Act.

Other sources increased the enrollment: the maturing baby-boom population reaching college age, economic good times, and growth in the state of California. Five new colleges would join the California State College system (for a total of 15) during these years. School teachers returned to college to meet new, higher credential standards. Locally, the school brought in students through outreach programs such as the Greater Humboldt Committee.

By 1955 campus leaders deemed it necessary to hold a Frosh Camp to orient freshmen before fall classes began. (This would become the Humboldt Orientation Program.)

To serve these new students, HSC offered Saturday morning classes and, for the first time, noon-hour classes. The college also called upon technology. In the spring of 1958, HSC used IBM punch cards for registration and grades.

The complexion of the student body changed. With an increase in the number of students from southern California — some spoke of organizing a Southern California Club — Humboldt was no longer a commuter school.

Men students outnumbered women two-to-one in 1955, a far cry from the "girls' seminary" a decade earlier. Nearly a third of HSC's students were over 25 years old.

HSC Exploits its Uniqueness

Humboldt State's curriculum expanded with the growing student body, as the school sought to define its niche in the CSC system. Historian Hyman Palais said President Siemens, when he visited Sacramento (and later Long Beach), took every opportunity to make a case for HSC's uniqueness. He lobbied for a field house because of Humboldt County's excessive rainfall. He argued for special equipment and facilities to support Humboldt's unique programs in fisheries, wildlife, and forestry. He requested an ocean-going vessel for instructional purposes. He lobbied for the marine laboratory which was eventually built in Trinidad.

By 1956 HSC had an entire natural resources division (headed by Charles Yocum) offering B.S. and M.S. degrees in fisheries and wildlife management. Within four years HSC added academic divisions for business (headed by William Jackson), language arts (John Pauley), biological sciences (William Lanphere), and physical sciences (Roscoe Peithman). The school offered new programs in industrial arts, political science, and — with the help of Eureka obstetrician and gynecologist, Ted Loring, MD — nursing. The forestry program, under the direction of Ed Pierson and Jerry Partain, expanded from a two- to a four-year professional forestry management curriculum. HSC also offered a master's degree in the liberal arts.

In 1956 a new general education program required all degree earners to take a minimum of 45 units in social science, natural science, literature, art (or philosophy), health and physical education, oral and written expression, and psychology. For those not wishing to specialize at the undergraduate level, a "group major," broadly cultural in character, combined the general education core with 36 upper division units in three academic subjects.

Humboldt kept up with the times with courses in Russian language and television and a 1962 lecture on "Opportunities in Computer Programming." CSC international programs for overseas study reflected an increasing social and cultural awareness, as did a federally funded Indian teacher education program. During the early 60s HSC took steps toward creating a Native American studies program.

California's Master Plan

In 1961 the state legislature transferred authority over the California State Colleges from the department of education to a newly formed board of trustees that would manage, administer, and control all 15 colleges, including Humboldt State. Chancellor Buell Gallagher headed the CSC system.

This change reflected an influential study published the previous year. *A Master Plan for Higher Education in California, 1960-75* made recommendations for coordinating the state's three tiers of higher education: the University of California, the California State Colleges, and the junior colleges. The report directed Humboldt State to emphasize "instruction in the liberal arts and sciences and in professions and applied fields which require more than two years of collegiate education and teacher education."

This report marked the beginnings of more rigid control over individual campuses. More structure, more reporting — and more bureaucracy.

"Old deans never die, they just lose their faculties."

Dean of Instruction Homer Balabanis headed a veritable employment bureau in this era, hiring more and more faculty to meet teaching demands and to replace a generation

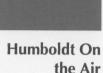

Humboldt On the Air

In the late 30s, John Van Duzer, professor of speech and drama, gave weekly music appreciation programs for children over KIEM radio. In the early 40s Don Karshner taught HSC's first radio classes. His students presented drama, interviews, recitals, and campus news reports on KIEM.

The programs were popular in the community. Eureka's station KHUM, coveting the student talent, claimed, "No one should be blessed with exclusive use of such a group." Soon student programming crossed the air over several frequencies.

After the war, Ted DeLay constructed a studio and wired up a campus sound system. Loudspeakers brought student programs to the quad, the dining room and the parking area. When Roscoe Peithman and his electronics class installed a carrier-current system in 1954, KHSC could be heard campus-wide. Its first broadcast schedule was under the direction of William Ladd.

This set the stage for KHSC-FM, which in 1960 became California's first state college radio station. Dale Anderson and George Goodrich developed the facilities, and John Rawlinson served as program manager. Gayle Karshner threw the switch 22 years later as KHSU-90.5 frequency, increasing its power to 100 watts, extending coverage to McKinleyville and Eureka.

In the years since, KHSU has extended its service area (northern Mendocino County to southern Oregon) and its reputation for diversified programming.

(*clockwise from top right*) The new cafeteria/student activities building; the new men's gymnasium, fieldhouse, and Redwood Bowl; workers at the Coop's fountain, 1960: Vera Walters, Dora Seiber, Lee Kenman, and Blanche Hendrickson.

A growing campus: *(clockwise from top right)* new library; new wildlife building; aerial view, Siemens Hall and Van Duzer Theatre under construction; Forestry Club president Peter Passof helps dedicate forestry building, 1962.

reaching retirement age. In 1955 he hired 26 new faculty; in 1958, another 36. By 1961 HSC had over 170 full-time and 20 part-time faculty.

Pop Jenkins, teacher at Humboldt for 38 years, retired in 1953 and passed away in 1955. Balabanis commented:

> Professor Jenkins was the most beloved professor in the history of the institution because of his interest in the individual student: not only in teaching them, but in their personal welfare.

Other respected, long-time faculty and staff retired, including Homer Arnold, Maurice Hicklin, Imogene Platt, Harry MacGinitie, and Myrtle McKittrick.

Among the newcomers who would make their mark on Humboldt State were Milton Dobkin (speech), Ken Humphrey (education), Leon Wagner (music), Wilmer Bohlmann (political science), John Borgerson (physics), Jim Carroll (sociology), Winn Chase (industrial arts), Glenda Richter (foreign language), Tom Clark (chemistry), Dick Day (English), Bob Dickerson (economics), John Gimbel (history), Ford Hess (physical education), James Householder (mathematics), Jack Schaffer (psychology), John Butler (biology), Robert Kittleson (economics), Richard Ridenhour (fisheries), Ralph Hassman (physical education), Bill Thonson (art), and Rudolph Becking (forestry).

There were many others, of course, some of whom still teach at Humboldt and some of whom retired in the 80s. Indeed, Humboldt's emeritus faculty now includes 170 members, as opposed to only nine in 1961.

Edifice Complex

Naturally, with all the new students on campus, shortages of classroom and laboratory space continued. New and newly-remodeled structures began to dot the campus. So did new sidewalks and landscaping projects.

Early construction projects included the wildlife management building, the art/home economics building, a new music building, the home management cottage, a speech arts/auditorium structure (now Van Duzer Theatre), and a new administration building (now Siemens Hall).

Upon completion of the new administration building in 1959, the old administration building was renamed Founders Hall to recognize the many persons responsible for establishing and operating Humboldt State. A ceremony honored those founders, thirty-one of whom found their names on a plaque mounted near the entrance. Three honorees attended the ceremony: Elenore Brizard Holcombe, Bernice Bull, and Len Yocom.

The changes on campus kept coming. The Green and Gold Room became a lounge and meeting room. A student health building, student activities center and cafeteria were welcome additions. Campus athletic facilities also saw great improvements: a new field house with tennis courts to the south, a men's gym (now the East Gym) and an indoor swimming pool. Redwood Bowl got a roof for the west stands, expanded seating (with lumber donated by local companies), and a rubberized track around the football field.

The year 1962 saw the science building expanded, the forestry building and the new library completed, the old library (now Van Matré Hall) remodeled into an engineering building, and a new education and psychology building erected (now Harry Griffith Hall).

Campus/Community Relations

A flourishing economy, a growing student body (patronizing local merchants), and winning football teams combined to strengthen relations between campus and community during these years. The dedication ceremony for Founders Hall, with its recognition of community support for Humboldt State, also strengthened bonds between town and gown.

The Hammond Lumber Company donated a truck to haul forestry students to and from the woods. For the price of one dollar, Pacific Lumber granted the College Improvement Association a twenty-year lease on land near Freshwater for use by the forestry department.

Many local merchants sponsored work scholarships for students and supported campus activities financially. By the early 60s, Humboldt State had the highest number of scholarships per student in the state system.

The active HSC alumni association sponsored a student loan fund. President Estelle Preston McDowell opened an association office in the campus Coop. For homecoming festivities in 1959, alumni came by train from as far away as the Bay Area. The following year a Who's Who award for distinguished alumni honored its initial recipient: George Hogan, class of 1933.

The HSC family helped out in the community during the Christmas flood of 1955. The school also produced an annual community Christmas concert. In 1960 HSC began allowing anyone living within the service area, including public school students, the privilege of using the campus library.

Athletics

In 1955 a new Sports Hall of Fame inducted 30s football star Earl Meneweather. Four years later the Hall of Fame inducted its first woman, 20s track star "Cinder" Elta Cartwright. The glory days of Humboldt athletics would not be limited to the past, however. As the college grew, so did the strength of its athletic programs. This growth would climax in a football bowl game for the small-college national championship in 1960 (see p 83).

HSC's first athletic trainer, Ced Kinzer, arrived during this era. So did Lucky Logger (1958), a nine-foot mascot replica of a Lumberjack. The Marching Lumberjacks abandoned their backwoods garb for more conventional uniforms in 1959. The first alumni-versus-varsity football game took place that year, with the alumni winning, 21-6.

Football coach Phil Sarboe (with knife) celebrates his finest season, 1960. (*l to r*) Hal Wood, UPI sports editor; Primo Marca, baker; and President Siemens.

Francis Givins coached the basketball teams from 1953-64. Robert Doornik coached HSC's first track-and-field champions in the Far Western Conference in 1959. Bill Hook was NAIA champ in the discus. Wrestling coach Gordon Schroeder's team won its first FWC championship in 1960.

But football boasted the most success. HSC had already won its first FWC championship in 1952 under coach Phil Sarboe. The Lumberjacks would have only one losing season in this era. Star players included George Psaros, Jim Ingram, Phil Huff, Earl Barnum, Charles McAnnick, Ceasar Fromma, Zeke Van Deventer, Ed White, Sal Sino, Manny Simas, Vester Flanagan, Fred Whitmire, Cecil Stephens, and Drew Roberts. Many received FWC and NAIA honors.

The 1960 season (11-1) capped off the Sarboe era. HSC ranked second nationally in the NAIA at season's end. Sarboe got NAIA coach-of-the-year honors. The defensive line built its reputation as the Green Chain.

Games had to be moved to Albee Stadium in Eureka to accommodate the thronging fans. Ten thousand attended the western regional playoff against Whitworth College. Victorious there, the Lumberjacks took their 20-game winning streak to St. Petersburg, Florida, to play for the NAIA championship in the Holiday Bowl. There, a controversial late fourth-quarter field goal by Lenoir-Rhyne College (North Carolina) pulled out a 15-14 victory.

Women's sports, while largely intramural, improved greatly after the arrival of Louise Watson (1953) and the other women's coaches: Kay Gott Chaffey, Elizabeth Stagle Anderson Partain, and Leela Zion. Star players in this era included Pat Clark, volleyball; Betty Larsen, badminton; and Ann Hitt and Karen Paulsen in basketball.

(clockwise) The traditional Sweetheart Ball, 1960; students of the early 60s learn television broadcasting; the costumes and madness of the Mardi (Muddy) Gras.

Paul Asp recalls that you couldn't get in to the 7:30 football games if you didn't have your seat by 7:00. Homecoming parades, he remembers, were huge events, with elaborate floats and five or six local high school marching bands competing for prize money.

Funding for women's sports came largely from proceeds from the Women's Recreation Association's ice cream machine in the gym (approximately $100 a year). Intercollegiate sports for women would have to wait several more years.

Campus Life: from Muddy Gras to the Great Potato Rebellion

Don Karshner became dean of students in 1954, a position he would hold for 17 years. He oversaw counseling, student activities, admission and registration, the health program, student council, the bookstore, and housing. During his tenure, faithful observance of traditional campus activities continued, but the increasing size of the student body dictated certain changes.

In 1954, out of a fear that HSC's growth would stifle its friendliness, the sidewalk west of Founders Hall was designated Hello Lane. For several years the proclamation of Hello Day meant students and faculty saying "Hi" to everyone they passed.

Romance may have been alive and well on campus, but the annual Sweetheart Ball was dropped for lack of interest in 1957. All-college assemblies had to be discontinued in

1958 for lack of space. The All-College Picnic, held each year until 1959, gave way to Lumberjack Days. Faculty and staff began holding a spring outing separate from the students: a salmon bake at Camp Bauer.

Homecoming continued amid much enthusiasm. Kate Buchanan, associate dean of students in this era, related an amusing anecdote about one particular homecoming. There was a lot of rah-rah and competition between the classes in those days. Sophomores had to try to light a bonfire set up by the freshmen. This particular year the freshmen, in collusion with the maintenance department, received permission to burn down an entire building, a state-owned house scheduled for demolition. "It was all hush-hush," Buchanan said. "[But] somehow news got out that the freshmen had a house to burn, so the sophomores burned down the house."

Trouble was, they burned down the *wrong* house! Buchanan feared deep trouble. As it turned out, the house the students burned down was *also* scheduled to be razed, thus avoiding a major catastrophe.

Flyer for the salmon bake at Camp Bauer, 1956: "All professors and other absent-minded persons get your tickets early . . . $1 per adult. Children 12 years old and under free. (Employees under 4 feet tall admitted free.)"

In special events, a time capsule burial (to be opened October, 2053) highlighted commemoration of the 40th anniversary of Humboldt State's founding. Campus Dedication Week, held in the spring of 1960 in conjunction with the annual Festival of Arts, celebrated the new master plan and new campus buildings, particularly Sequoia (now Van Duzer) Theatre. One ceremony introduced a new HSC flag. The presidents of all the state colleges attended.

Kate Buchanan: Hard Work & Humor

When Art Dalianes arrived in 1955, new semesters started with freshmen being received in the campus homes of faculty and administrators. He was assigned to Kate Buchanan, who had come to HSC in 1946 as assistant professor of English and Speech. Dalianes remembers her as a person whose door was always open, for *any* student. Following Eugenia Loder, she became dean of women (a title that would be changed to "associate dean of activities"), and helped overturn the rule that females could not wear slacks.

Art would eventually be student body president and later Kate's assistant ('60-64). During this era he, Kate and Don Karshner developed the concept of a campus activity center. "Think big," was Buchanan's motto. "If you think small, you limit your visions."

Kate always saw the bright side and turned negatives into positives with her humor which made any assignment fun. She helped lay the groundwork for the University Center where a meeting room is named for her. She organized the Phoenix Club to support older, single women returning to college.

Dalianes remembers when he and Don Peterson — they had been in charge of the infamous bonfire that burned down the wrong house — had to go in to face Kate the morning after the fire. His heart was pounding because he had so much respect for Kate and felt so badly about what he had done. At first she sat quietly at her desk. Then she looked up and burst out laughing. "That's one for the books," she said.

And now it is.

Wildlife and Conservation Week continued, and other observances joined it: Religious Emphasis Week in 1954 (although by 1963 religious services associated with graduation would disappear); American Heritage Week, 1957; and Marriage Education Week, 1958.

Students organized for forensics, an annual Business Day, a Veterans Club (with Happy Hours once a month at the popular restaurant, the Big Four), and an International Relations Club (with an annual dinner for foreign students). Dramatic and musical productions remained popular including *King Richard II, The Madwoman of Chaillott,* and *Humboldt '56.*

Fads included holding apple cider chugalug contests at Lumberjack Days, gyrating in hula hoop contests, dancing the twist, and sunbathing at College Cove. Faculty members often participated in the merriment. In 1956 Professor Leon Wagner quipped on the Elvis Presley rage:

> There was a young chap from Tupelo
> Who caused all the girls loud to *yell-o;*
> With his lips and his *hips,*
> He'd no need of *quips*
> The teenagers' hearts all to *swell-o.*

Students elected professors Ralph Roske and Lyn Pauley as king and queen of "Muddy" Gras in February, 1956. They held an Ugly Professor contest in 1961, nominating James Gast, Jean Stradley, Ralph Roske, Don Karshner, Ralph Samuelson, Charles Bloom, and Phil Sarboe.

The 1958-59 *Handbook for Nelson Hall Women* included these popular song lyrics:

> We're the girls from Nelson Hall
>   you've heard so much about;
> Mothers lock their sons up
>   whenever we go out;
> You've heard a lot about us
>   and most of it is true;
> All the fellows fear us —
>   we hope you fear us too. BOO!

With the 1959 completion of Sunset Hall for women and Redwood Hall for men, HSC began requiring unmarried students under 21 to live either on campus or at home. Enforcement became increasingly difficult, however, with nearly 2,000 students enrolled in the fall of 1959.

With living space harder to come by, fraternity and sorority houses made a comeback: Delta Sigma Phi, Tau Kappa Epsilon, and Delta Zeta. Off-campus students took advantage of a Metro Bus Service begun in 1962. Twenty shuttle rides between campus and the Arcata Post Office cost $4.

By 1958-59 the Associated Student Body budget topped $80,000. Football receipts and student activity fees (doubled to $10 in 1958) were the chief sources of revenue. In 1961 ASB built a new student activities center (part of the present University Center), with cafeteria, bookstore, and ASB offices. The ASB relinquished control over food services, the bookstore, and vending machines to Lumberjack Enterprises, a nonprofit corporation of administrators, faculty, and students.

Everything but a Centerfold

Several campus publications sprouted during these years. *Toyon*, a literary journal, first appeared in April of 1954 and continues to this day. *Hilltopper*, a magazine devoted to the nonfiction interpretive article, made its appearance in 1957 under the editorship of Chloe Higgins DeBrunner. The Forestry Club began publishing *Annual Ring* in 1959. Editor John Bell noted that he and his staff "included just about everything except a Playmate of the Month."

Forum appeared in 1961, an iconoclastic, off-campus publication unauthorized by the administration. Editorial staffer Todd Collins said they aired important contemporary issues in order to nurture an active concern in the student body. Those issues included compulsory student body cards, anticommunism, and racism. *Student Statesman*, equally controversial but ultraconservative, also circulated on campus.

A Growing Discontent

These latter publications may have represented the beginnings of a growing student discontent. After the shock of the Kennedy assassination in 1963, controversy and activism would increase still more, and discontent would characterize the late 60s.

How times had changed. As recently as 1953, a caustic, satirical *Lumberjack* column, "Pierre the Legionnaire," had actually provoked a student vote to determine whether such "profanity" should continue. An example of Pierre's (a.k.a. Jack Norton) wit:

> If you have Spaid, you have it made:
> And then there's Pauley, take care not to folly.
> But look out for "Mac," here you need tact.
> And Marx who's hard, wait 'til you see the card.
> Oh, you have Smith for lab,
>   take care you'll end upon a slab.
> And Karshner, well,
>   nothing rhymes with Karshner.
> Don't be nervous — see you all in the service.

A more daring discontent soon became apparent. By 1959 students were addressing the alleged opposition of the administration to free student expression. Students demanded participation in campus governance and control over contents of *The Lumberjack*. This led to an ad hoc commission on student rights and responsibilities.

In the early 60s, men students began wearing beards. By 1963 women students were violating the rule that slacks be worn only on days of inclement weather. A *Lumberjack* columnist charged, "The rule is being honored mainly in the breeches."

In 1963 when cafeteria meal tickets increased to $250 per semester, 17 students were disciplined for "The Great Potato Rebellion," so named for great quantities of mashed potatoes tossed around the cafeteria. Faculty spokespersons criticized "the uncalled for, uncitizenlike outburst of student behavior."

Another incident, involving somewhat more consequential weaponry, prompted President Siemens to ban firearms (loaded or not) from the dormitories.

Looking Outward

The pages of *The Lumberjack* chronicle Humboldt students' growing interest in off-campus issues.

Tackling Segregation

excerpts
from an article by
Carol Harrison
in *Humboldt Stater*

In December, 1960, with the civil rights movement in its infancy and segregation commonplace in the South, an undefeated Humboldt State football team boarded a plane for St. Petersburg, Florida, to play for the national championship . . . Upon landing, its five black members were whisked away to housing quarters separate from the rest of the team.

The trip focused nationwide attention on the tiny North Coast campus, but it also awakened the conscience of a faculty, a community, and a state. Thirty-seven faculty members sent the following telegram to the superintendent of public instruction:

. . . Humboldt State College, in accepting a bid to appear in the NAIA Holiday Bowl . . . has accepted segregated housing facilities for the football team. We wish to know . . . whether there is any policy relating to state participation in segregated events. . . .

The story hit the national news wires. Everyone could read about the segregation controversy. Stuck in the middle, far from home, were players who only wanted to cap off their perfect season with a national championship. "We felt it was 33 guys from Northern California against the world," fullback Ed White said.

The ire of St. Petersburg came down on the team. The *St. Petersburg Independent* reminded "discontented athletes" that the city maintained the same laws for "such highly paid and extremely respected men as Elston Howard and Hector Lopez of the New York Yankees." At home, the 37 faculty members were tagged by the *Humboldt Times* as "agitators." Professor Kathryn Corbett offered a different perspective.

They were all our kids, and you knew them all ... I was incensed that boys in my class weren't going to get the same treatment when they were going to play on the same field....

Coach Sarboe met with the entire team and made it clear that if there were a single objection, the team would not play. They did play, losing 15-14 to North Carolina's Lenoir-Rhyne College.

"As it turned out, going and the telegram were the best things possible," Ed White said. "We had earned a shot at the title. I would have been highly upset if we hadn't gone, no doubt. But the controversy initiated changes that had to be made."

Bill Love, who, with teammate Dave Littleton, was active in the civil rights movement, said, "No change ever occurs without some cost. Our sacrifice might have been the end of the world for us, but it's nothing compared to the ultimate sacrifice people paid for that same cause."

83

(clockwise from top right) **Aerial view of 1957 campus; baccalaureate services in the Founders Hall courtyard; the long lines during registration.**

During McCarthy's Red Scare, the question arose whether instructors should be allowed to discuss communism in the classroom. Students voted in the affirmative. They also expressed concern for world conflicts: Arabs vs. Israelis, the nuclear arms race, U.S. involvement in Southeast Asia, and relations with the Soviet Union and Communist China. In 1957 they raised funds for the Hungarian Relief Fund.

The Cold War was heating up. After news of Sputnik, Humboldt students debated whether the Soviets led the U.S. in science. The Berlin crisis of 1961 caused mobilization of the local National Guard unit, 40 percent of whose members were students. That crisis, plus the 1962 Cuban missile crisis, created growing concern over the possibility of nuclear war. Industrial arts students designed a home-style fallout shelter. Throughout the community — throughout the country — citizens packed their basements and closets with emergency food, water, blankets, and flashlights.

Environmental issues cropped up, too. Students complained that dams on Northern California rivers would hurt trout and salmon fisheries. The *Lumberjack* rang with both preservationist and conservationist views — a reflection of the growing polarization of politics in Humboldt County.

When the Kinsey Report on sexual behavior came out, a poll showed some students feared it would lower moral standards while others looked forward to reading it. In other campus polls, students objected to the loyalty oath required for an NDEA loan. They petitioned the state legislature to end the death penalty. One married student, denied access to the delivery room at local hospitals, chained himself to his pregnant wife.

An Activist Faculty

Certain faculty members of this era, like their students, showed signs of increased activism. The local chapter of the Association of California State College Instructors often led the way.

In 1959 ACSCI joined student protests over the loyalty oath requirement for NDEA loans. Later that year, when the state forced HSC to implement its first parking fee ($13 per semester), students and faculty alike protested. ACSCI supported professor James Householder, who parked behind Founders Hall without a permit. His primary objection was that fees were not used locally to improve parking facilities. Householder lost his case in court but received only a suspended $25 fine.

After the 1960 master plan vested more power in the hands of the chancellor, other organizations became more vocal in the interests of faculty rights and work benefits. Chapters of the following organizations began to rival ACSCI for leadership on campus: the American Federation of Teachers, the California Teacher Association, the California State Employees Association, the California College and Universities Faculty Association, University Professors of California, and the American Association of University Professors.

In 1961 the faculty organized the first academic senate to "provide an efficient organization for the fullest participation of the faculty in the development and review of local educational policy." That first senate consisted of President Siemens, faculty president Fred Telonicher, four academic deans, and 18 elected faculty representatives. Edward Steele chaired the senate which established committees of faculty-elected members, including one to recommend reappointments and tenure, and another for promotions. In 1963 Humboldt sent faculty delegates Hyman Palais and Roscoe Peithman to the first statewide academic senate for the CSC system.

Two controversies in 1960-61 focused attention on HSC faculty. The first involved the petition to boycott the Holiday Bowl game because of racial segregation (p 83). While controversial both in the South and on the North Coast, the publicity proved effective. The next spring the NAIA announced that the Holiday Bowl would move from St. Petersburg to Fresno.

That didn't stop the controversy at home. *Lumberjack* editorials criticized those faculty members who

> waited virtually to the eve of Humboldt State's greatest football game, when the college was in the national limelight for perhaps one of the few times in history, to stir up an embarrassment for the team, the coaches, the administration, and Humboldt State.

Editor Hugh Clark wrote further:

> We are unhappy and disgusted with 37 members of our faculty who we think have done wrong . . . We believe their actions so close to game time had a marked effect on the team, and we charge them with hurting HSC's chances in the Holiday Bowl . . . Never will we forgive them for hurting Humboldt State and a great bunch of guys who deserved considerably better.

A second controversy occurred when members of the political science department were charged with being communist sympathizers. The accusation followed publication of Professor Ross Koen's book, *The China Lobby*, which criticized Chinese Nationalists and their U.S. supporters. A southern California assemblyman stated, "Humboldt County is the most subversive county in the state." Assemblyman Frank Belotti from Humboldt County defended his constituency, and Governor Edmund Brown and President Siemens called the charges irresponsible.

That 1960-61 school year appeared to diminish the cordial relations between faculty and students. *Lumberjack* editorials marked the loss of friendliness. They claimed faculty members had stopped attending student social functions as before. In February, 1961, for example, no faculty king or queen reigned over Muddy Gras.

Perhaps students and faculty could feel small-college friendliness slipping away. These, however, were only the beginnings of disaffection and controversy. The *real* 60s had just begun.

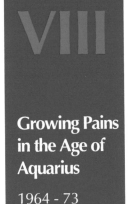

Growing Pains in the Age of Aquarius

1964 - 73

The Times

Joe College was dead. At least, his obituary (p 88) had been written. A new era called for a new kind of student. This was the dawning of the Age of Aquarius. All the old stereotypes, all the old rules and values, were up for grabs.

As early as 1963, *Lumberjack* columnist Rod Mitchell had urged HSC students to

> Doubt! Dissent! Refuse to accept eternal verities! Make fun of Arthur Schlesinger! Poke holes in Dan Smoot! Read Karl Marx! If you want to make a perfect ass of yourself dancing the stomp, have at it!

A 1971 letter to the editor, however, expressed one alumnus' disgusted reaction to all the turmoil on campus:

> Just Old Fashioned
>
> When I was a student, I was quiet,
> I didn't protest and didn't riot.
> I wasn't unwashed, I wasn't obscene;
> I made no demands on Prexy or Dean.
> I sat in no sit-ins, I heckled no speaker;
> I'm forced to admit, with some hesitation;
> All I got out of school was an education.

The late 60s and early 70s saw both increasing campus activism and increasing polarization. President Siemens, in his second decade, watched Humboldt State suffer through severe growing pains. World and national incidents during the Johnson and Nixon years triggered student and faculty activism far more visible than at any time during the college's history. Student government and campus organizations grew restive.

Meanwhile, enrollment increased threefold and the number of faculty fourfold. The close-knit camaraderie between faculty and students diminished. Relations between campus and community grew strained.

Students vote to strike in response to the Cambodian incursion, May, 1970.

Vietnam & the Draft

After the shock of the Kennedy assassination, controversy and activism increased on campus. While Beatlemania invaded the dorms in 1964, a more substantial controversy brewed over establishment of Redwood National Park. This would create a schism to endure for years. Still, though environmental issues provoked continuing local interest, it would be the draft and the war in Vietnam that would dominate the late 60s and early 70s.

Anti-draft sentiment paralleled increased U.S. involvement in Vietnam. Picket signs around an Air Force recruiter in 1966 read: "Declare War on Poverty, not Peasants." That December, campuswide seminars focused on Vietnam. "Teach-ins" covered draft issues. In 1967, 120 students and professors observed National Stop the Draft Week, sponsored by Students for a Democratic Society.

In Memoriam: Joe College

editorial by Mike Stockstill in *The Lumberjack,* January 14, 1970

The end of a decade and the beginning of a new one cause people to look back and reflect on the events that made history. Perhaps the 60s will be remembered as the decade of death. John and Robert Kennedy, Martin Luther King, Lee Harvey Oswald, each one murdered in a terribly public manner. But one death during the 60s went largely unnoticed. Perhaps it was because the exact time, place, and cause of death is not really known. However, the deceased is gone forever — Joe College is dead.

Who was Joe, anyway? Most of us would probably have recognized Joe when he was around. He was the "Big Man On Campus" leading the cheers at the rah-rah pep rally before the Big Game. He could be seen gladhanding his way around campus in his flashy clothes. At the Big Game, Joe was there with his blanket and wineskin, radiant in the innocence of the all-American girl next to him, who wore his pin. After the game Joe went over to the frat house or down to the Keg to quaff a few beers.

In student government, Joe was the first to complain at the SLC meetings that school spirit was really lagging. Joe was pleased when student government acted on important matters like selection of cheerleaders and new uniforms for the band. In class, Joe was the typical student, going for the gentleman's "C" and no more. He took his notes, read his books occasionally, and crammed religiously for his finals.

But there was another Joe College too, probably more typical than the one just described. This Joe went to class, studied, went to the games, drank some beer now and then, got his degree, and left college without so much as a whisper in his four years of education. This Joe College was no wave maker. He was content to float along the current of college life, avoiding the swirl of controversy, the responsibility of involvement, the disappointment of self-realization.

In the end, though, Joe College met his fate. The Big Game wasn't so big anymore, life at the old fraternity house became little more than beer busts and rank initiations, and suddenly, life began to blow up all around him — the bomb, politics, race riots, Vietnam, the crisis of the environment. Joe died of being irrelevant to the world around him.

Now that Joe has gone, a new generation has come to take his place. Like all new generations, they came in with a roar, caused some excitement, made some mistakes, and learned some lessons. Now they will begin to grow up. Their causes are just; their era is beginning.

Rest in peace, Joe.

88

During 1968-69 HSC was conflict-ridden to the point where some feared the campus would be destroyed. In response to faculty/student strikes and rowdiness, Governor Ronald Reagan threatened "expulsion of students or the dismissal of teachers who interfered with the educational process." Chancellor Glenn Dumke threatened to take over CSC newspapers because of the use of four-letter words and nude photographs.

A Student Conduct Program for Humboldt State College, issued in 1968, attempted to "avoid the combat zone atmosphere on many of the nation's campuses." A Smith River retreat in 1970 brought together administrators (including President Siemens), faculty, students, and members of the community. The retreat promoted a sense of community and addressed issues of mutual concern. All this preceded the Cambodian Incursion in May of 1970 and the resultant outburst of turmoil.

The high points of anti-Vietnam War protests occurred during 1969-70: Vietnam Moratorium Day, the Cambodian Incursion protest, and the closing of campus in May of 1970. Leading up to these events, the Peace and Freedom Party and Students for a Democratic Society had been organizing pacifist activities since 1966. At the other end of the ideological spectrum, the Two Per Cent Club and the John Birch Society had organized counterdemonstrations and combated communism on campus. Before the fall of 1969, however, many students remained uninvolved.

Then came Vietnam Moratorium Day, October 15, 1969, endorsed by President Siemens and the academic senate. Vice president Milt Dobkin cites this as evidence of Siemens' ability to adjust to changing conditions while at the same time keeping things under control. Approximately 800 students gathered in the Sequoia Theatre (now Van Duzer Theatre) to hear speakers protest U.S. involvement in Vietnam. Participating faculty members included Ken Hallum, Tom Jones, and John Hennessy.

Students decided to communicate their concerns to the community, and the demonstration moved to the Arcata Plaza. More antiwar speeches filled the air, including one by the campus chaplain, Father Gary Timmons. No violence occurred, and students met with a positive reception from much of Arcata.

That next spring, however, President Nixon announced that the U.S. had invaded and bombed Cambodia — in contradiction to his 1968 campaign promises to wind down the war. A more volatile situation arose. Across the nation, campuses became scenes of mass demonstration, violence, and even bloodshed at Kent State and Jackson State.

At Humboldt the Student Legislative Council met in special session on May 6, 1970, in the Sequoia Theatre Plaza. A crowd of more than 1,100 observed the 13-1 SLC vote "to demonstrate the students' commitment against all war and all violence." Suggestions included the banning of Lumberjack Days (or renaming them "Peace Days"), a boycott of all student activities, and flying the American flag upside down until the war ended.

On May 11 nearly 3,000 students, faculty, and administrators gathered again on the Sequoia Quad with an open mike for speechmaking. Students voted for a voluntary, peaceful, one-week strike. They then canvassed door-to-door in Arcata and held a teach-in at Arcata High to gain community support. Students with long hair trimmed their locks so as not to offend local citizens. President Siemens called for abolition of the draft system and condemned the Cambodian Incursion.

Governor Reagan responded to Cambodian protests and strike threats around the state by closing all CSC and University of California campuses, including Humboldt.

President Siemens, professor Tom Jones, and two students, funded by $8,000 raised on and off campus, traveled to Washington to speak to the California delegation in Congress. *The Lumberjack* reported,

> Formerly bearded professor Jones attended the rally with face clean-shaven and a military haircut to facilitate communication in Washington.

Another rally upon their return allowed Siemens and the others to recount their reception by the California delegation. They believed their expressed opposition to the Cambodia incursion and the Vietnam War had had an impact.

So while the traditional Lumberjack Days and a miniskirt contest went forward in late May, other HSC students were sending 600 draft cards to the Princeton Anti-Draft Center to be forwarded to Washington.

Antiwar and antidraft activities did not disappear after that, but the intensity died down. Activism on this front virtually ended in 1971 with suspension of the draft, a significant reduction of American involvement in Vietnam, and with 18-year-olds receiving the right to vote.

Other Activism

A change in the celebrities visiting campus reflected the new political climate. At one point the CSUC board of trustees reprimanded HSU for engaging in left wing politics almost exclusively.

In the early 60s Humboldt County had welcomed Harry Golden, Barry Goldwater, Ronald Reagan, and Chuck Yeager. But between 1968 and 1971, Robert Kennedy, Ladybird Johnson, Herbert Marcuse, B.F. Skinner, Dick Gregory, Dick Tuck, Ralph Nader, Willie Brown, Tom Hayden, and James Farmer visited HSC. Oregon senator Mark Hatfield spoke against the draft. Representative Allard Lowenstein of New York spoke against the war and President Nixon. On the other side of the issue, Ronald Reagan spoke at College of the Redwoods in 1970. Because of the heckling, Reagan vowed he would never speak on another college campus.

College students across the nation were growing more active politically and more critical of educational institutions they attended. The University of Michigan and UC Berkeley became leading centers of criticism of American society. Humboldt State also felt those trends. By the late 60s, conflict abounded between students and administrators/faculty.

Associated Students demanded student participation in campus policymaking. Students demanded, and received, a nonsmoking section in the cafeteria. They protested the arrests of hippies and the suspension of high school students for wearing long hair. They supported legalization of marijuana and prostitution. They called for enrollment of more ethnic minority students. They balked at computerized registration. They criticized faculty members for being unwilling to devote more time to them. They lodged protests against letter grades and demanded student membership on faculty committees.

The service organizations Circle K, International Knights, and Spurs dissolved. Meanwhile students formed a Black Student Union, a chapter of the Sierra Club, Sisters of Sappho, Gay Peoples Union, Jewish Student Union, the HSU Caucus for Women, a Stop-at-Four committee (four traffic lanes on Highway 101 through Arcata), and MEChA. The campus began hosting Black Culture Week, Asian-American Awareness Week, Women's Awareness Week, Third World Week, and a Safe Hitchhiker's Workshop. Speakers representing the Student International Meditation Society invited students to "expand the mind without drugs."

By 1970 *The Lumberjack* was calling for "a move away from campus-centered activities to more community and political projects and issues." In that spirit, homecoming was abandoned. The battle was joined in the controversy over Redwood National Park. Environmental Awareness Week raised student consciousness, as did debates on zero population growth and women's liberation issues.

On the other hand . . .

The Underground Guide to the College of Your Choice, published in 1971, labeled Humboldt State College as the nicest of the California State College campuses. The publication stated: "There is a lot of long hair and beards here, but the straights are the majority."

"Straights" and traditional social activities did continue, for the most part, right through the stormy 60s. Students selected a homecoming queen, Delta Sigma Phi Dream Girl,

Don Karshner: Dean of Students

In its first 50 years, Humboldt State, like most American colleges, took a paternalistic attitude toward students. Faculty advisors took over in planning student schedules. Dorm directors acted as surrogate parents. ASB sponsored only administration-approved events.

Sensitive to the changing times, Dean of Students Don Karshner saw students as responsible adults. In the 50s, Karshner tried to set up a student judiciary body. In the 60s, he guided student/administration negotiations over a new student conduct program that redefined the roles, getting rid of *in loco parentis*. This led to the peer group concept and visitation rights in the dorms, better interracial situations, and student participation on various college committees.

When the Vietnam War incited campus protests, Karshner helped students find peaceful avenues for venting their frustration. He established a free speech stump. He encouraged a door-to-door canvass to break down stereotypes between "long hairs" and local citizenry. He fostered Gentle Days — singing, dancing, joyous human encounter — and community service through Youth Educational Services.

In the protest march to the Arcata Plaza, Karshner worked with students and police to avoid confrontation and riot. He also convinced President Siemens to take the students' case to Washington. This helped relieve the confrontational aspect of local protest.

Karshner was not alone in recognizing the changes sweeping across America. With or without the dean, students and administrators might have reached new understandings about rights and responsibilities. But the HSC family of that generation gives Don Karshner much of the credit for a smooth and positive transition.

Don and Gayle Karshner, in the 60s, outside their home on 16th Street, now used for classrooms and offices.

91

(*clockwise from top right*) Original ITEP students, 1969; Volkswagen stuffing, 1965; Professor of Education, Harry Griffith, for whom the education/ psychology building is named; John F. Kennedy memorial, 1963.

92

(clockwise) Marine lab site dedication at Trinidad; Professors George Allen and James Gast, pilot, aboard the *R.V. Sea Gull*; Humboldt County landscape during the 1964 flood; Fern Lake, located in the forest near Redwood Bowl.

and sweethearts for Tau Kappa Epsilon, Sempervirens, and the Freshman class. They shelled out from $2.40 to $3 for a cafeteria meal ticket. They dropped a quarter in the vending machine slot for a Coke. They flew home over the breaks (a one-way flight to San Francisco was $31). They planned Sneak Day at College Cove.

A big celebration in 1963-64 marked HSC's Golden Anniversary. Distinguished alumnus Monroe Spaght delivered a special address on "Concern for Character."

Student Life in the Age of Aquarius

However, the times they were a-changin'. *Sempervirens* (yearbook) and *Hilltopper* ceased publication. The pornographic film, *Behind the Green Door* showed at the University Center. The last two fraternities, Delta Sigma Phi and Tau Kappa Epsilon, dissolved for lack of interest. The Athenaeum on campus began selling beer and wine to students and faculty.

In 1970 students elected their first African American ASB president, Bill Richardson. The Student Legislative Council eliminated the homecoming queen election, partly due to lack of interest, and partly because in 1972 a goat and a pig were entered as candidates.

With the new dorms in the Jolly Giant area (p 99) came new ideas for student living. Prompted by student demand, Ed Simmons, associate dean for activities, and Dave Murray, assistant director of housing, brought forward the peer group concept. Students assumed more responsibility for their own living conditions.

Beginning in 1968, student Living Group Advisors replaced adult chaperones. Residents made their own rules and regulations. Some dorms allowed co-ed visitations on Saturday and Sunday afternoons. In 1969 all dorms became co-ed. By 1971 the residence halls allowed alcohol for those 21 or older. (The two most popular student haunts, however, remained off campus: Flynn's Inn and The Keg.)

Also new to the late 60s: miniskirt contests (Bobby Tracy won in 1969); Hare Krishnas; the first annual Intercolle-

giate Kite Flying Contest (at Clam Beach); a Humboldt Honeys club; an oceanography publication, *Pacific Oceanic Olio* (1965); the Clam Beach Run (1966); the annual Humboldt Film Festival (1968); an all-male pep band, the Golden Berets (1968); and a culture fair (1969) sponsored by the Third World Coalition.

Associated Students' active Student Legislative Council started a college union fund in 1965 to support construction of a new activities center, completed in 1973. They established a Speakers' Stump on the commons and helped sponsor a tutorial program in the local public schools. They organized Youth Educational Services (Y.E.S.) in 1968 and in 1970 returned control of *The Lumberjack* to the journalism department.

In 1964 the SLC threatened to picket academic senate meetings unless they got representation on faculty committees. Two years later they called for more student free choice, self-rule, and "the right to be consulted by administrators on all policies involving students." In 1969 the academic senate and President Siemens officially accepted student representation on 37 campus committees.

Athletics

A *Lumberjack* editorial in 1971 called for spending less ASB money on athletics, spending more on "worthwhile" activities, and charging students full price for attendance at sporting events. Two years later, some suggested abandoning the Lumberjack as the mascot because it excluded women, conservationists, and Native Americans. Throughout this era, just a few hours' drive south of the campus, a generation of flower children called for peace and love.

On the other hand, hard-hitting Lumberjack football remained one of HSC's most visible and successful extracurricular programs in this era, led by the school's two most successful coaches, Phil Sarboe (1951-65) and Frank "Bud" Van Deren (1966-85). Sarboe won or shared in five Far Western Conference championships before retiring in 1966. In 1968 Van Deren's team won the conference and went on

Humboldt International Film Festival

David Phillips, who received a B.A. at HSU in theatre arts with film emphasis, established the Humboldt International Film Festival in 1967 — the oldest student-run festival of its kind in the world.

Beginning in 1968, student and independent filmmakers across the planet began submitting super 8mm, 16mm, and 35mm films: documentaries, animation, narratives, and experiments. They entered for the public exposure, but also competed for cash prizes and a few more dubious awards: the Pavlov's Dog Award, for instance, or the Banana Slug and Cinematic Disobedience awards.

More than mere entertainment, the film festival provides an educational forum for student and independent filmmakers. As the festival has grown in prestige, it has brought in world renowned judges — Lynn Kirby, Les Blanc, Marcia Lucas, Frank Capra, Bill Nichols, and Jan Krawitz — who have shared their career experiences and insights into this creative art.

Preserving a National Treasure

Tom Parsons, a social psychologist and former Peace Corps volunteer, spent 19 years (1968-87) with local tribal elders developing an easy-to-learn phonetic alphabet, and putting the Karuk, Hupa, Tolowa, and Yurok languages into writing. The tribes then compiled textbooks documenting their history, music, prayers, dances, and craft techniques.

This was the American Indian Languages and Literature Regeneration Project, a joint effort between the university, the federally-funded Center for Community Development, and Native Americans. CCD received numerous commendations for recognizing and preserving a national treasure before its extinction.

CCD (now the Center for *Indian* Community Development) has helped hundreds of programs over the years. Parsons and his successors have facilitated the projects, then gotten out of the way. Projects arose from needs felt within the community, rather than being imposed by outside "experts."

Projects have included an annual symposium on the status of women, the Northwest Indian Cemetery Protective Project, the Humboldt Senior Resource Center, the Humboldt Recreation Program, agricultural development and marketing, a cultural and trade exchange with China, development of Braille community signs (the raised symbols beside elevator buttons, for instance), and the Humboldt Bay Brass Society.

Student Marian Mooney and Tom Parsons at CCD, 1985.

to beat Fresno State in the Camellia Bowl. Stars of those years included Carl Overstreet, Tom Waters, Carl DelGrande, Ted Snapp, Mel Oliver, Frank Vulich, Jim Costello, Jeff Getty, Dan Hook, Danny Walsh, and Len Gotshalk. John Burman received the Northwestern California Athlete of the Year award from USC's Heisman Trophy winner, O.J. Simpson.

Don Clancey and Robert Anderson with a flood of applications for admission, 1970.

Track, coached by Lynn Warner and Louise Watson, won first place in 1964. Warner's 1969 team won the Women's Recreation Association track and field meet in Redwood Bowl. Janet Niece, Janet Ferguson, Georgia Becker, Sheila Perkins, Jacque Deaner, Lynn Forson, Barbara Perkins, Pat Wold, and Beverly Wasson starred.

The Lucky Logger Society — Bill Caldwell, Fred Duerr, Kit Freeman, Chuck Moser, Tom Nelson, and Rick Stromberg — cheered them on. So did the Marching Lumberjacks, who added hard hats to their uniform after 1968. Maria Johnston became their first female member in 1972. Referring to one of the band's common antics, she said, "I could drop my pants like any guy; I even have a pair of boxer shorts."

In cross-country and track and field, Gary Tuttle, Bill Scobey, Pete Haggard, Larry Cappel, Mike Bettiga, and Fred Lioni starred. Trained by coach Jim Hunt, Tuttle and Scobey became NCAA national champs. Three top golfers in the late 60s were Larry Babica, Greg Bean, and Bob Clark. Wrestling coaches Ralph Hassman, Bud Van Deren, and Bob Kelly tutored several individual champions: Al Hagerstrand, Jerry McPherson, Tim Fox, and Ed Johnson. In swimming and water polo, coached mostly by James Malone, stars included Mike Morey, Marshall Kane, Eric Oyster, Ted Deacon, and Tim and Ken Cissna.

Ced Kinzer (1954-68) stands out as Humboldt's most successful baseball coach (235 wins against only 146 losses). Dick Niclai (1965-75) coached the basketball team; Larry Kerker (1957-69), tennis. A soccer team began intercollegiate competition in 1972 under Robert Kelly.

Women athletes played intramural sports primarily. They also competed with two- and four-year colleges in the Extramural League of College Women. The league sponsored various Sports Days for hockey, volleyball, and basketball.

HSC women began competing in the Northern California Women's Intercollegiate Conference in 1969. For three seasons Barbara van Putten's volleyball team won the championship. By the early 70s, women were organizing for intercollegiate competition and conference play on a level comparable to men's sports.

Population Explosion

On the Sequoia Plaza, students may have argued zero-population-growth issues, but for the school as a whole, enrollment exploded — far faster than administrators had anticipated. The major increase came from community college transfers and students outside the area. In the fall of 1969, enrollment surpassed 5,000. Administrators placed a lid on enrollment because of the lack of facilities and housing. More than 10,000 students applied for admission in 1970; only 1,600 were accepted. Still, by 1973 enrollment stood at 7,053.

The state master plan predicted 10,000 full-time equivalent students for Humboldt by 1980 and 12,000 by 1990. Arcata citizens were concerned that the community could not absorb these numbers. They drew up plans for the college to expand east and north, so as not to further affect Arcata residential patterns. HSC's 1970 master plan called for an elaborate, decentralized student housing complex and outdoor facilities for the natural resources program in those locations. As it turned out, Humboldt contained its growth and did not reach the predicted numbers.

Campus Expansion

New buildings sprouted up all over campus. These included the auto mechanics building (1966), a child development laboratory (1968), art and music additions (1969), a new building in the biology complex (1971), a natural resources sciences building (1972), the Joseph M. Forbes Physical Education Complex (1973), the marine laboratory in Trinidad (1966), and, with student funding, a new University Center (1973).

Founders Hall, the oldest building on campus, underwent remodeling in 1969-70. Kerr Tower was added, a meditation room named for donors William, Dorothy, and Guy Kerr.

College Elementary School closed in 1970, marking the end of on-campus laboratory schools in the CSC system. It signified, as well, increased efforts to place teacher credential students in community schools for classroom experience. The CES (now Gist Hall) was remodeled to accommodate nursing, speech and hearing, and media center facilities.

In 1973 Humboldt leased the vacant Trinity Hospital on 14th Street and relocated personnel and payroll offices, the post office, HSC Foundation, and other services. This became known as the university annex.

Student housing shortages plagued the school. Arcata Hotel rented student housing at $10 per room per week in 1967. Humboldt Village I, a trailer park for men established in 1967, was the first new housing since 1959. Eight dormitories and a commons in Jolly Giant Canyon opened in 1968, as did Humboldt Village II. Cypress Hall followed in 1973. The housing shortage continued, however. *The Lumberjack* reported a student living in a teepee on a ranch on Fickle Hill. Rumor had it that students were living in hollowed-out trunks of redwood trees.

Products of the Great Society

The mid-60s saw Lyndon B. Johnson's Great Society and increased emphasis on federally funded social programs. Several of those programs came to the aid of HSC students.

The Department of Agriculture extended its food stamp program to low-income college students in 1963. The Federal Economic Opportunity Act of 1964 provided work-study funds for needy students. In 1966 Upward Bound began allowing lower-income high school students to spend summers experiencing college life. A Cold War G.I. Bill in 1966 further encouraged enrollment at the college level.

The Peace Corps, a Kennedy program, found ripe recruiting on campus (and continues to do so). By 1964, twelve former HSC students were serving in Africa and Latin America. Volunteers in Service to America (VISTA), Lyndon Johnson's program for a domestic peace corps, began recruiting after 1965.

The Center for Community Development, established under the Higher Education Act of 1965, promoted the use of college and university resources in the community to direct expert attention at local problem areas. Under first director William Murison, the CCD sponsored programs ranging from a seminar on concrete technology to a program on preschool children to three Christmas plays for Ferndale and McKinleyville. Several years later, Tom Parsons began a Native American language restoration program to preserve the Karuk and Hoopa tongues.

Campus/Community Disharmony

Community/college relations had been cordial in the early 60s, but tensions interfered near decade's end and into the 70s. According to Milt Dobkin, town and gown relations began deteriorating about the same time Humboldt was celebrating its Golden Anniversary (1964). With HSC salaries now larger than those in the local economy, community volunteerism and support diminished. College of the Redwoods also drew away some support.

The many nonlocal students and faculty coming into the area caused friendliness to drop off, particularly in Eureka. Some of these newcomers supported ideas which were unpopular in the local community. In 1965 professors Rudy Becking and Pat McGlyn formed Citizens for a National Redwood Park, which drew the ire of the timber industry.

New buildings
on campus:
(*clockwise*) music
building, 1969;
University Center,
1973; Cypress
Hall, student
housing, 1973.

Recognition of
the HSC football
team's NCAA
Regional Cham-
pionship success in
the Camellia Bowl.
(*l-r*) Team captain,
quarterback Jim
Costello, Arcata
City Councilman
Ervyl Pigg, and
Coach Bud Van
Deren.

In the early 70s, much of the HSC community supported a ban on teepee burners. (Before finding profitable uses for wood chips, timber companies used teepee-shaped incinerators for burning scrap material.) One teepee burner was located just north of the campus. The college's opposition provoked antagonism in the timber community.

Complaints also arose over the excessive noise from a popular student hangout, The Keg (now Hunan's), where Arcata was introduced to the Motown sound. Students didn't endear themselves any further by opposing a new freeway on Highway 101 which, they charged, would eliminate student housing. They also opposed the Butler Valley Dam project and the building of a motel at the Bayside Cutoff.

Now that the right to vote extended to 18-year-olds, community members feared the college might dictate local policies and elect its own candidates. Indeed, at ASB president Arnie Braafladt's urging, six of ten candidates running for Arcata city council in 1972 came from campus. Forestry professor Rudolph Becking and student Alexandra Carlin Fairless were elected, presumably through campus voter support. The mayor of Arcata responded by declaring the image of HSC "very poor."

But the community probably exaggerated campus influence in elections. Two campus candidates won, yes, but only a third of the eligible voters on campus had bothered going to the polls. And though the Butler Valley Dam project lost by two-to-one, analysis of the vote suggested widespread opposition, not just from students. (At least in environmental issues, campus and community worked together more and more for their mutual benefit.)

Concerned community and campus leaders worked hard to minimize abrasion. A city/college liaison committee discussed shared problems. The North Arcata Merchants Association sponsored HSC Appreciation Day in 1965. In 1967 community members lent substantial financial support to athletics through Lumberjacks, Incorporated.

Reaching out to the community, HSC students helped victims of the great 1964-65 flood. The women's gym housed National Guard and army personnel during that disaster.

Associated Students helped the community through twelve Youth Educational Service programs, such as Big Brothers and Big Sisters, aid for disabled children, and tutoring. The Forestry Club completed a trail through Arcata's Redwood Park in 1969. Students cleaned up the highway between Arcata and Eureka. And in 1971, "long hairs" rode with local police on patrol in order to improve relations between students and law enforcement officers.

Faculty Matters

While the 1961-62 catalog listed 75 full-time members, ten years later 355 full-timers were listed. Prominent among the new members added during that decade:

Art — Bill Thonson, Bill Anderson, Demetrios Mitsanas, Stuart Sundet
Biology — John DeMartini, Robert Rasmussen, Richard Meyer, Gary Brusca
Business — Don Lawson
Chemistry — John Hennings
Economics — John Grobey
Engineering — William Schenler
English — Bob Burroughs
Forestry — Brooks Sibley
Geography — John Coleman
Geology — Frank Kilmer, John Longshore
History — John Hennessy, Frank Mahar
Industrial Arts — Frank Jolly
Journalism — Mac McClary
Library — George Magladry, Erich Schimps
Mathematics — Victor Tang, Roy Ryden
Music — Phil Kates, Joe Farruggia
Physical Education — Jim Hunt, Evelyn Deicke, Fred Siler
Physics — Fred Cranston
Political Science — Ilie Smultea
Psychology — Dennis Musselman
Speech — Peter Coyne, Lewis Bright
Theatre Arts — Jean Bazemore
Wildlife — John Hewston

Father Gary Timmons became college chaplain in 1968. He and Ed Simmons, associate dean of activities, would later launch the popular Simmons-Timmons Think-In for dorm students.

While many new faces came on campus, long-time faculty and staff retired as well, including Homer Balabanis (40 years); Fred Telonicher (40); John Van Duzer (31); William Lanphere (30); Helen Everett (28); Bill Johnson, chief of plant operations (27); Kate Buchanan (22); and Ivan Milhous (21). Harry Griffith, professor of education since 1939, died of a heart attack in 1966.

Milton Dobkin

This major turnover changed the complexion of the faculty. The increased numbers challenged any efforts for all-campus faculty gatherings. Despite the president's persistent efforts, the close-knit familiarity, informality, and friendliness diminished.

Faculty organizations, generally vocal critics of CSUC policies, criticized Governor Reagan's 1967 budget cuts and proposals to charge students tuition. Faculty held teach-ins on Vietnam, the draft, and CSUC policies.

Math professor James Householder led an unsuccessful crusade against campus police carrying guns. He declared: "When peace is maintained by force, I say it's a different kind of peace."

Another burning issue was student representation on the 1973 presidential search committee (allowed by the academic senate after an initial negative vote). Professors accommodated in the Mai Kai apartments protested deteriorating office conditions by wearing hard hats to faculty meetings.

Administrative Changes

Homer Balabanis retired in 1964, after forty years as professor, dean, and finally vice president for academic affairs.

The college began a lengthy game of musical chairs to find a permanent successor, culminating in the hiring of Milton Dobkin in 1969. Dobkin had first come to Humboldt in 1955 to teach speech communications before leaving to work in the chancellor's office in 1966.

Dobkin's tenure coincided with major changes in HSC's academic organization. The former nine divisions became five schools and one division:

School of Behavioral & Social Sciences
Houston Robison, dean
School of Creative Arts & Humanities
Ronald Young, dean
School of Business & Economics
Jesse Allen, dean
School of Natural Resources
Donald Hedrick, dean
School of Science
Roscoe Peithman, then
Raymond Barratt, dean
Division of Health & Physical Education
Larry Kerker, dean

President Siemens established new administrative offices, too: dean of graduate studies (Alba Gillespie); dean for undergraduate studies (Whitney Buck); dean for academic planning (Richard Ridenhour); dean of administrative affairs (Donald Strahan); dean of students (Don Karshner); business manager (Frank Devery); and ombudsman (Thomas Stipek). HSC football star Earl Meneweather became ombudsman and special assistant to the president in 1971: the college's first African American administrator.

Other appointments, beginning in 1972, reflected increased attention to fairness for ethnic minorities and women. Bobby Lake became ethnic affairs assistant. Jack Norton directed Native American studies. Kathryn Corbett coordinated the new affirmative action program. Donald Armbrust, Susan Frances, and Helen Batchelor followed in that position.

Academic Changes

The number of degree programs remained steady (59 in 1961; 65 a decade later) despite the growth in student population. By 1967 the most popular majors were forestry, wildlife management, biology, psychology, and history. A nursing program and Asian studies joined the curriculum in this period.

As the numbers of school-aged children mushroomed nationwide, demand for teachers increased. California's Ryan Act in 1970 replaced elementary and secondary teaching credentials with multiple- and single-subject credentials. This gave an interdisciplinary thrust to the waiver program and created curricular changes in many departments, especially education and English.

In other academic changes, commencement ceremonies moved to Redwood Bowl in 1966 to accommodate the larger graduating classes. HSC switched from semesters to a quarter system in 1967. Class registration by computer began in 1968 (though HSC offered no computer classes yet). A Ship or Sink committee obtained the *R.V. Catalyst,* a seaworthy vessel for oceanography, in 1970. Also that year, College of the Redwoods took over the junior college program, and an HSC Cluster College began fulfilling general education requirements.

University Status

In 1971 President Siemens accelerated his personal crusade to gain university status for Humboldt State. Such a change, he argued, would give the institution prestige, would help in recruiting faculty, and would promote the centerpiece of Humboldt's unique curriculum: natural resources.

In June, 1972, the school officially became California State University, Humboldt. In the fall of 1974 that cumbersome title was reduced to Humboldt State University.

End of the Siemens Era

University status represented the last major accomplishment of President Siemens. Within a year he announced his retirement, effective September, 1973. Milt Dobkin, vice president for academic affairs, served as acting president until the next July. John Pauley, professor of theatre arts, was acting vice president.

Siemens' tenure as president had lasted 23 years. He led Humboldt through its major period of growth, both in enrollment and physical facilities. His many accomplishments included developing a nationally prominent natural resources program, great strides in academic freedom, and university status.

Historian Hyman Palais used numbers in adding up the Siemens years, 1950-73. Siemens arrived at a small college with 57 faculty and 650 students operating on a half-million dollar budget. The campus comprised 21 buildings, only five of which were permanent. He retired from a university with almost 500 faculty, over 7,000 students, an operating budget of almost $16 million, and a campus comprising over 70 buildings, approximately 30 of which were permanent.

Oden Hansen, former dean of campus development, saw Siemens' major achievement in his promotion of the physical attractiveness of the campus. "The Campus that Cornelius Built" reflected the president's passion for flowers, gardening, and aesthetic landscaping.

No Cinderella Story

1974 - 87

While the early 70s had reflected a confidence and combativeness, Humboldt's mood gradually took on a more chastened, conservative tenor. The school looked to resolve shrinking budgets, declining enrollment, and the remnant social and political tumult born of the late 60s. For many, job consciousness surpassed social consciousness. Watergate, inflation, the Iranian hostage situation, and a retrenched federal government came to bear.

President Alistair McCrone

A new president would guide the university through these years. Alistair McCrone succeeded Cornelius Siemens in 1974. McCrone earned a Ph.D. in geology from the University of Kansas. (His wife Judy is also a geologist.) His credentials included teaching at New York University and serving University of the Pacific as academic vice president, and as acting president.

President McCrone announced his feelings about the arts and humanities. He said, "The liberal arts are the very center of our culture." He wanted to create at Humboldt an educational experience equivalent to that of a small liberal arts college.

He would become known for his emphasis on academic excellence and his willingness to delegate authority. In an age of limited growth and a limited pool of college-aged people, he urged the faculty to work toward quality of education rather than quantity. He also urged better community/university relations.

A 1977 presidential commission on the nature and potential of HSU, chaired by biology professor Richard Meyer, made five comprehensive recommendations:

President Alistair McCrone

1) develop non-state funding to supplement declining budgets;
2) maintain a balance between breadth and depth of curriculum, and retain the liberal arts nature of Humboldt State University;
3) improve faculty morale through increased opportunity for research and creative activities, faculty exchange, faculty development, and funding for undergraduate travel to professional meetings;
4) divide the labor when assigning faculty to research, teaching, advising, or governance;
5) improve a sense of community within the campus and between the campus and the North Coast community.

The work of the commission reflected the president's intent to serve as a catalyst, releasing existing talents in the faculty and staff.

No Cinderella Story

Despite these efforts, Humboldt State, once labeled by the *L.A. Times* as "the Cinderella of the North," for the first time in decades felt more like one of the ugly stepsisters. Two decades of steady growth came to a halt in 1974, as applications and enrollment declined.

College applications were down statewide. Humboldt's dropped by 50 percent. From 7,053 students in 1972-73, enrollment plunged to 5,843 in 1986-87. The decline particularly affected sociology, history, and other behavioral and social sciences.

The end of the draft, general uncertainty about employment, and a shift from liberal arts to vocational education contributed to the trend. State funding declined, and student fees increased accordingly. Annual registration fees jumped from $348 in 1982 to $699 in 1984, and $910 in 1988. These fee hikes, combined with federal government cutbacks on NDEA student loans, further aggravated the declining enrollment. And this, in turn, brought renewed anxiety over faculty and staff layoffs.

Fighting Back:
Recruiting & Retention Efforts

Robert Hannigan, dean of admissions, records and school relations, and Chris Muñoz, director of admissions and school relations, guided new efforts to recruit and retain students. An enrollment planning and management task force got faculty and staff visiting high schools around the state. Tele-Student sent them to the phones to encourage prospective enrollees. Admissions adopted open enrollment for students over age 30 and gave incoming freshmen priority for dormitory housing. The recruiting of ethnic minority students became — and remains — a priority.

As for retention, the Humboldt Orientation Program, student affirmative action (focusing on retention of ethnic minorities), the AIR Center's advising, and spring preregistration all contributed positively. Student services sponsored Club Faire to involve students more deeply in campus life. A new course, Exploring and Developing Goals for Education (EDGE), helped freshmen without declared majors.

Golden Handshakes

In spite of having fewer students, the university was still considered overstaffed according to state formulas. By 1977 nearly every new faculty member was hired on a temporary basis and assigned a teaching service area (to establish priorities in the event of a layoff).

The CSU authorized a Golden Handshake in 1980, allowing a two-year service credit toward retirement. This encouraged older faculty and staff to step aside to protect the positions of young colleagues. Forty-seven Humboldters

took advantage of the plan, helping the school avoid layoffs. Faculty retired in sufficient numbers to spur Kathryn Corbett to form a Emeritus Faculty Association in 1985.

Among the long-time faculty and staff persons retiring during these years: William Jackson (36 years), business; Robert Kittleson (25), economics; Jean Stradley (27) and Joe Trainor (21), education; Frank Wood (32), French; John Gimbel (24), history; Art Stegman (28), industrial arts; Leland Barlow (37), Charles Fulkerson (36), and Dave Smith (28), music; Kay Chaffey (32), Joseph Forbes (26), Ced Kinzer (22), Jim Hunt (21), and Ralph Hassman (19), physical education; Roscoe Peithman (31) and Fred Cranston (23), physics; Eugene Flocchini (37), accounting officer; Virginia Rumble (34), secretary to the president; Don Karshner (35), dean of student services; Joe Noga (25), plant operations; Frank Devery (23), business manager; and Don Strahan (22), vice president of administrative affairs. Two others of long service died: Larry Kerker (25 years), physical education, and Wilmer Bohlmann (23), political science.

Faculty Representation

Faculty organized statewide to protect themselves against a variety of threats: layoffs; post-tenure review or an end to tenure altogether; students on appointment, tenure, and promotion committees. The liberal University Professors of California preferred a systemwide strike, while the conservative California Faculty Associations promoted collective bargaining.

In 1978 the state legislature authorized collective bargaining. A statewide vote determined CFA would handle that bargaining. CFA's first contract with the CSU had minimal effect on working conditions. It did, however, create $2,500 Meritorious and Professional Promise Awards, perceived by some as indirect merit pay increases.

To build local morale and promote faculty research, President McCrone established the HSU Institute for Research and Creative Projects in 1980. Theodore Ruprecht directed it. In 1984 the president sponsored a one-day conference, "Reflections on the Future." Faculty and administrators contributed ideas on HSU's strengths and weaknesses. After some mentioned a lack of recognition for faculty research and scholarship, the Scholar of the Year award (appendix G) came into being in 1986.

Morale still slipped. Professor Todd Young surveyed 80 faculty members who perceived themselves overworked and underappreciated. Much of their disgruntlement stemmed from years of "bean counting" (student enrollment numbers). Also, the switch back to semesters, after nearly twenty years on the quarter system, was producing mountains of extra work: curricular revision, new requirements for majors and minors, and the tiresome conversion of quarter units to semester units for all continuing students. The changeover also disrupted personal routines by beginning the academic year in late August in order to complete the fall term before Christmas.

On the Administrative Side . . .

Considerable administrative turnover occurred during these difficult years. Chancellor Glenn Dumke, the cornerstone of the California state universities and colleges, retired in 1982 after 20 years (nearly the entire existence of the California master plan). He turned over the reins to Ann Reynolds, a biologist and former provost at Ohio State.

Milt Dobkin retired in 1983, having served HSU nearly 25 years, first as professor of speech, then as vice president for academic affairs, with a year as interim president. In his tenure, Dobkin promoted the consultative process and served as spokesperson for the faculty. He established faculty participation on key committees and encouraged innovative teaching.

Michael Wartell succeeded Dobkin. President McCrone described Wartell as a change agent. To the five existing schools (renamed colleges in 1982) Wartell now added two new colleges — the college of health and professional studies, and the college of visual and performing arts. He brought new deans into the academic structure, and he eliminated the interdisciplinary studies and special programs division.

College of Health, Education & Professional Studies
  Bette Lowery, dean
Teacher Preparation Programs
  Sheila Webb, assistant dean
College of Behavioral & Social Sciences
  Lee Bowker, dean
College of Business & Industrial Technology
  Lee Badgett, dean
College of Science
  James Smith, dean
College of Humanities
  Ronald Young, dean
College of Visual & Performing Arts
  Robert Everding, dean
College of Natural Resources
  Richard Ridenhour, dean

Concern for social fairness advanced with the 1979 appointment of Linwood Wall to direct special support programs (Upward Bound, Educational Opportunity Program, veterans services, and the children's center). The next year, disabled student services and a state-funded student affirmative action program began.

A drop-in Academic Information and Referral Center, under the leadership of Lolly Haston Quackenbush, improved academic advising. The revamped alumni association was placed under Jim Hamby, director of the HSU Foundation.

Edward Del Biaggio replaced Frank Devery as business manager, then replaced Don Strahan as vice president for administrative affairs. Edward "Buzz" Webb followed Don Karshner as vice president for student affairs. Don Christensen replaced Michael Corcoran as director of university relations.

Lionel Ortiz replaced George Preston directing plant operations. Athletic director Frank Cheek was followed first by Dick Niclai, then Chuck Lindemenn. Claude Albright took over for Earl Meneweather as ombudsman. Robert Hannigan replaced Robert Anderson as dean of admissions and records. Donald Wilson succeeded university librarian Donald Koepp, then was himself succeeded by David Oyler. David McMurray became director of student health and

(*clockwise from right*) A class held in the Founders Hall courtyard; Presidents Cornelius Siemens and Alistair McCrone at the dedication of Siemens Hall; greenhouse dome; engineering and biological sciences building, 1982.

counseling services. Jan Petranek became director of development. Thomas Nelford, executive assistant to the president, was succeeded first by John Hennessy, then by Alba Gillespie.

Building Projects

The removal of Humboldt Village and the university takeover of the Mai Kai apartments for faculty office space created a serious shortage of student housing despite the declining enrollment. Some students' parents would buy homes in the community, rent them to other students, then sell the homes upon their child's graduation. Many students stayed in local campgrounds or slept in vans.

Tightening budgets restricted campus expansion, but several construction projects did alter Humboldt's appearance. Additions included an all-weather soccer field where Humboldt Village had been (1979), an all-weather field in Redwood Bowl (1979), an engineering and biological sciences building (1982), and a geodesic greenhouse (1982).

From 1975-77 Founders Hall, the health center, Gist Hall, the marine lab, and the library all underwent remodeling or expansion. Later in this era, geology occupied a remodeled lower level of Van Matré Hall and the wildlife program received a new aviary.

In 1976, on the eastern edge of campus, the U.S. Department of Agriculture completed its redwood sciences laboratory of the Pacific Southwest Forest and Range Experiment Station. Since 1963 this station had been conducting silviculture, watershed management, and fisheries research in association with Humboldt's natural resources programs.

An arsonist's fire gutted the forestry building in 1979, leading to a costly rebuilding. Cypress Hall shut down in 1980 for repairs on the unstable hillside behind the dorm. When a ceiling collapsed in a Founders Hall classroom during the 1981 Thanksgiving holiday, the entire building's ceilings had to be reinforced before classes could resume. Structural problems in the new engineering and biological sciences building forced closures for repairs over several years.

During this era it might have appeared as though any building not under construction or repair was at least undergoing a name change.

> College Elementary School — Arthur S. Gist Hall (1972)
> Faculty Club — Women's Center (1973)
> Art/music/theatre — Homer P. Balabanis Complex (1974)
> Sequoia Theatre — John Van Duzer Theatre (1975)
> Administration — Siemens Hall (1978)
> Music recital hall — Charles Fulkerson Recital Hall (1978)
> Education/psychology — Harry Griffith Hall (1978)
> Marine lab — Telonicher Marine Laboratory (1979)
> Engineering — Van Matré Hall (1980)
> Child development — Swetman Child Development Lab (1980)
> Language arts — Theatre Arts Building (1980)
> Lounge in the University Center — Karshner Lounge (1980)
> Nelson Hall meeting room — Goodwin Forum (1980)
> UC all-purpose room — Kate Buchanan Room (1981)

At a 1973 auction, the president's home (no longer the actual place of residence) sold for $60, a visible end to the era when presidents lived on campus.

Curricular Trends

Reflecting the mood of the nation, Humboldt shifted away from its liberal arts toward a more back-to-basics approach. The multidisciplinary Cluster Program, for instance, was dropped for lack of interest in 1980. The CSUC began requiring entering students to take a basic Entry Level Mathematics Exam. All graduates had to pass a Graduate Writing Proficiency Exam.

By 1976, history had fewer than 100 majors (compared to 400 in 1970) but forestry had more than 600. By 1982, business had the most majors (716) and was offering a Master of Business Administration degree.

The natural resource fields showed renewed vigor in the mid-70s, reflecting both the job market and society's growing environmental sensitivity. A new master's degree emphasized ecology and environment. Humboldt dropped civil engineering in favor of environmental engineering. Native American Career Education in Natural Resources was funded by the U.S. Department of Health, Education, and Welfare.

The College of Natural Resources suffered a setback in September of 1978 when the research vessel *Catalyst* sank on a voyage to Crescent City. The crew escaped injury, but oceanography suffered the loss of equipment. The next year Harold Sherwood of Marina Del Rey gave the university a new vessel, *Malaguena*. According to professor James Gast, the new vessel did not quite meet departmental needs. It was sold and the funds used to outfit *S.T. 893*, an 88-foot vessel once owned by the U.S. government.

Other curricular changes during these years included a revised general education program; the addition of ethnic studies, women's studies, and Native American emphasis programs; a credential in handicapped learning; a M.S. degree in multicultural education; a liberal studies degree in child development; and a major in computer information systems.

New technologies affected academics. The Center for Appropriate Technology opened shop in Buck House. The library implemented an automated barricade system. By 1977 over 200 courses used computers, even though the computer information systems major didn't follow until the 80s.

HSU made a trial run of a decimal grading system in 1976 but abandoned it for a plus/minus letter-grade system. To fight grade inflation, all activity courses became mandatory credit/no credit in 1977.

In 1982 HSU granted a record 1,174 bachelor's and 144 master's degrees. These were conferred at six separate commencement exercises: one for each college and the division of health and physical education. President McCrone had initiated this practice in 1975 to make commencement a more personal affair for graduates and their relatives.

Arsonist Guts HSU Building— Could Take Years to Replace

For 17 years the Humboldt State forestry building stood, but it only took 45 minutes to reduce it to rubble. And now it could take up to three years to rehabilitate the home of one of HSU's best known and most widely respected programs. The building, which burned early Saturday morning, is being called the victim of arson.

This fire was "man-caused and done on purpose," said state arson and bomb squad investigator Monty McGill late Monday after two days of probing through the ashes.

Scorch patterns indicate a flammable liquid was spread on the floor of the building. As of Tuesday, there were no suspects. Estimates of damage range from $1-3 million.

from an article by David Greenwald,
Arcata Union, January 30, 1979

A Reputation for Academic Excellence

In 1982 a national publication listed HSU among the top 31 "lesser known but of high quality" institutions in the U.S.

Several programs in particular gained recognition far beyond the local community. Political science initiated an internship program with government agencies in 1974. Thirty-one students participated in a Guatemalan interdisciplinary program, "Challenge of Change in Latin America," in 1976, and Career Development began its own cooperative education program in 1977.

A theatre major, Haig White, won the American College Theatre Festival award in 1981 for two plays he wrote. Micki Goldthorpe won a national award for her play, *Conversations of My Mothers*. A 1984 production of *Getting Out* qualified for presentation at the National American Theatre Festival at the Kennedy Center in Washington, D.C.

In 1982 both *The Lumberjack* and radio station KHSU gained recognition at the California International Press Association convention. The forensics team, led by Joe Corcoran and Janet Randor, placed 13th at a 1983 national meet in Utah. Forestry students won three straight conclaves in the early 80s, with Ray McCay chosen best logger in 1983. Karen Wyatt and Robin Schneider won in the women's division. Conservation Unlimited also won first in its conclave.

Trends in Student Life

The nation, including HSU, moved away from the combative political environment of the Nixon years to the more conservative, apolitical trend of the Carter and Reagan years. The end of selective service, the disillusioning Watergate scandal, and the energy crisis of the mid-70s had their impact. Student activism on certain issues continued, but by the end of this era most male Humboldt students were clean shaven and short-haired, and men and women were wearing trendy clothes. Many even voted for Reagan. Nostalgia for the 50s showed in the revival of homecoming, the yearbook, and fraternity/sorority traditions.

ASB president Eddie Scher conceived a Great Humboldt Spirit Celebration for the 1979 homecoming. He promoted full community involvement in the parade, bonfire, dance, and beer-bean-and-bread feed. Two 1917 alumni, Jessie Turner Woodcock and Harry Wandling, were chosen king and queen.

Lumberjack Days traditionally had been celebrated in June, but the 1986 conversion to a semester system meant the school year ended in May. To allow this social event to help acclimate new students to the university, Lumberjack Days moved to the fall.

Yearbooks, published between 1982 and 1985, renewed a tradition that had ended in 1966. Greeks reappeared on campus: Lambda Sigma Nu sorority sisters joined the frat boys of Delta Sigma Phi and Chi Phi.

Fads of the era included rock climbing at Patrick's Point and Moonstone Beach, skydiving, hang-gliding, jogging, jazzercise, skateboards, frisbees, hacky-sack, punk and New Wave rock-and-roll, backpacking, health foods, Killer Elite in the dorms, and mud wrestling. The Keg, a hangout since 1958, closed in 1977.

To educate and entertain the student body, various celebrities appeared on campus: singers Linda Ronstadt, Ricky Nelson, and Etta James; jazz musician Woody Herman; film producer Frank Capra; journalists Carl Bernstein and Tom Wicker; evangelist Jed Smock; writer David Halberstam; political activists Tom Hayden and Linus Pauling; physicist John Cofman; actor William Windom and Native American actor Will Sampson.

In 1974 two students streaked the library carrying "Impeach Nixon" and "Free the Dorm 1200" banners. *The Lumberjack* opined:

> To demonstrate how advanced our generation is, we have shunned childish fads and adopted more mature behavior patterns — like trotting around in the nude.

But even though the sexist nature of bared legs would lead to the demise of Lumberjack Days' miniskirt contest, many deemed streaking (bare everything) socially acceptable as a unisexual activity. College Cove soon became a nude beach.

Patterns of social behavior ebbed and flowed. Reports of alcohol and drug consumption, loneliness, and sexual activity all on the rise led the dorms to form a Social-Emotional Climate Committee in 1977. The health center director recommended condoms be sold in the bookstore, and family planning became part of the campus counseling services.

But at the same time, there was a rise in the popularity of religion. Christians handed out Bible tracts at the Univer-

CCAT

The Campus Center for Appropriate Technology was created in 1978 when students retro-fitted a neglected house on campus. They designed and implemented alternative waste, heat, water, food, and electrical systems. The new — or sometimes old, but always appropriate — technologies conserved precious resources and were kind to the environment.

Today CCAT is a fully functioning demonstration household. Visitors on guided tours see the house's thermal curtains; walls painted with non-toxic enamel; a 12-volt refrigerator and Freon-free cold box; a composting toilet; a wood-burning stove with internal heat exchanger; an herb garden and apothecary; a rainwater catchment system; wind turbines; a solar thermal water heating system; an office clock running off the electrical energy of two potatoes; a solar oven; a stove made of clay, sand, flour, and sugar — and more.

(*clockwise from top right*) Mrs. Judy McCrone and President Alistair McCrone at the President's Ball; Librarian David Oyler and retired librarian Helen Addison Everett at the dedication of the Everett Reading Room in the library, 1978; aftermath of forestry building fire,1979; late 70's May Day celebration.

sity Center quad. Almost everyone knew the Reverend Karl Bietz, who "witnessed" on the quad nearly every day for more than two years. A 1977 poll by the campus organization for Latter Day Saints reported 62 percent of the students had "a definite concept of God." George Walker in continuing education reported a similar finding two years later. *The Lumberjack* remarked,

> The presence of Bible studies, prayer groups, religious speakers, and cultural movies at HSU appears to be evidence that God is not dead.

Yuppies & Preppies

Going into the early 80s, student social life and outlook grew appreciably more conservative, more "yuppie" and "preppie" in orientation.

Three examples from 1983: 1) a "Dress for Success" workshop claimed clothing can determine how far one goes in a career; 2) professor John Grobey organized a student Republican Club to combat the "liberal, one-sided treatment of things" (in 1990 they would publish *College Republican* newspaper); 3) a *Lumberjack* column claimed the class of '83, unlike counterparts of the previous two decades, represented the philosophy "not to do anything that doesn't feel good."

Liberal rallies still drew good crowds— as protests against draft registration, South African apartheid, American involvement in Nicaragua, and the kidnapping of former journalism professor Alann Steen by terrorists in Beirut. Liberal *Lumberjack* editor Adam Truitt was suspended in 1986 in an ongoing controversy over whether CSU newspapers could endorse political candidates. And two years after the first AIDS Awareness Week (1986), condoms were sold in cigarette machines. In the main, however, conservative values prevailed in the 80s.

The Reagan Redwood Memorial Grove & Other Student Government Matters

This era's Student Legislative Council was less conservative than the students it represented. The SLC hesitated in funding athletics, forensics, and more traditional activities. It did, however, support nontraditional student services: a day care center for children, a crisis intervention referral center, a rape crisis center, Humboldt Women's Shelter, car pooling (when the price of gas went up), and subsidies to Arcata-Mad River Transit and Humboldt Transit Authority in return for lower student bus fares. The ASB focused on the needs of disabled students. Youth Educational Services bought an orange-colored van, "Orangeaid," to chauffeur disabled students around campus.

In 1976 Governor Ronald Reagan made the statement, "A tree is a tree. How many do you have to look at? Seen one you've seen them all." The SLC responded by dedicating the Ronald Reagan Redwood Memorial Grove — a lone redwood tree near the Highway 101 off-ramp on 14th Street.

Environmental issues captured student passions. The SLC supported expanding Redwood National Park. Group of Organic Alternatives to Toxic Sprays (GOATS) formed. Ralph Nader spoke on campus about decommissioning nuclear power plants. Students observed Sun Day to promote solar power. Others protested the destruction of whales, environmental policies of the Reagan administration (and Secretary of the Interior James Watt), and offshore oil drilling.

Meanwhile Native Americans demanded a Native American studies program and opposed celebration of America's bicentennial in 1976. Geography and geology students protested faculty hiring procedures. Gays picketed for rights and recognition. ASB withdrew from the state associated students organization.

ASB president Tom Bergman urged students not to register for the draft, which was reinstated in 1980. Antidraft rallies were less intense than the antiwar rallies a decade before. Ben Sasway, however, made national news as one of the few to refuse to register for the draft. He lost his case in court and received a two-year prison sentence.

These examples of activism notwithstanding, the tone of student government began to mellow. Many controversies of the early 70s had been resolved. Others needed little in the way of activism, as they were now mainstream social issues commanding significant public support.

As student government mellowed, participation waned. In the 1976 SLC elections, only six candidates ran for eight positions. Of 537 ballots (from more than 7,000 eligible voters), 180 were invalidated (Donald Duck and Richard Nixon, for instance, received write-in votes). Several SLC members resigned, feeling student government wasted their time. *The Lumberjack* opined: "Apathy is once again running rampant throughout student government." ASB president Jeff Lincoln proclaimed in 1981 that HSU student government would devote its attention to campus issues rather than national or international. This so aroused the student body that the 1982 ASB election was postponed for lack of candidates.

Athletics: Belt-Tightening

Intercollegiate sports experienced difficult times. If *Lumberjack* coverage and attendance figures are accurate indicators, athletics did not command much student attention until the 80s. Declining budgets and increased expenses caused athletics to tight up its organization and drop those sports considered too expensive: for men, baseball, swimming, water polo, and tennis; for women, tennis.

Athletic directors Frank Cheek and Chuck Lindemenn produced a more effective administration and improved HSU's competitive efforts. Lindemenn established an athletic advisory committee. He also hired Mike McKelvey, Vern Henricks, and Tom Trepiak to promote intercollegiate sports and organize fundraising. A series of sports banquets featuring celebrity speakers drew attention to the program. Over the years, the celebrity list would include Joe Kapp, Jim Plunkett, Steve Young, Bill Walsh, and George Blanda.

Support increased noticeably. Better publicity (and stronger teams) sold more season tickets and put more of the student population in the stands. Women's teams became competitive. Men's wrestling, cross-country, and basketball experienced success. Coverage in *The Lumberjack* increased. Cheerleaders reappeared at football and basketball games.

Women's Sports

A new women's gym (as part of the Forbes Complex) and a new women's conference boosted women's intercollegiate sports. The greatest boost, however, came through Title IX of the Federal Educational Amendment of 1972, which caused a major funding shift in favor of women's athletics.

Humboldt joined the Association of Intercollegiate Athletics for Women in 1974, competing in the Northern California Intercollegiate Conference. When Marilyn Taylor qualified for nationals in the two-mile run, she became the first Humboldt woman to compete in a national event since Elta Cartwright in the 20s.

In 1977 the women's teams joined the Golden State Conference. Five years later the Golden State Conference schools merged with the men's Far Western Conference schools to become the Northern California Athletic Conference. The competition level moved from NCAA division III to division II, with league competition in basketball, cross-country, softball, swimming, track, and volleyball.

Under Barbara van Putten and Lynn Warner, the softball team fared well, finishing as conference co-champions in 1983. Warner received coach-of-the-year honors in 1978 and 1983. Star players included Barbara Renaud, Kim Kohlmeier, Sue Harris, Deanna Allen, Debra Hinger Ford, Elaine Frakes, and Cheryl Clark.

The volleyball team, also under van Putten, won first in 1973, with a 7-1 record. Debbie Hungerford, Lorraine Schaffer, Alison Child, Jane Eilers, Cheryl Clark, and Kim McCleary starred.

Dave Wells' cross-country team placed third in the Golden State Conference two years in a row and second in the NCAC in 1984. Sheila Moskovich, Claudia Bergsohn, and Kathy Dolan starred. Track teams fared less well, but individual stars emerged: Sue Grigsby, Carrie Grover, Michelle

Betham, Liane Guild, Tori Belig, Donna Garrell, Kathy Dolan, Joann Poggi, Sheryl Fairchild, Cindy Hicks, and Tammi Callahan.

Betty Partain's swimmers did well individually, with their best season in 1976-77. Swimming stars included Sue Rodearmel, Grace Brosnahan, Karen Menne, Anna Marie Miller, and Anna Chong.

Women's basketball struggled for respectability under a series of coaches, including Diann Laing, Cinda Rankin, and Chris Conway. Laing's 1977 team took second in the conference. Christi Rosvold, Ticia Ledbetter, and Lisa Domenichelli starred.

Men's Sports

Wrestling and cross-country led the way for men's sports. Coach Frank Cheek's grapplers won the Far Western Conference five times between 1977 and 1981. They ranked second and third nationally in 1977 and 1978. Star wrestlers included Pat Stone, Doug Stone, Brent Wissenback, Mike Fredenburg, Marty McNellis, and Eric Woolsey. Woolsey went on to coach the 1981-82 team, receiving coach-of-the-year honors when his team finished second.

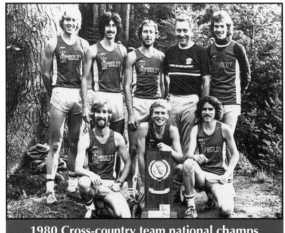

1980 Cross-country team national champs (NCAA Division II title).

Frank Cheek resumed coaching in 1983, with his wrestlers winning the conference title another three times. Eric Tessley, twice an NCAA division II all-American, won the national title in the 142-pound class in 1985. Steve Meckel, Dave Navarre, Dale Delaney, Don Dodds, and Rod Prnjak also starred.

Coach Jim Hunt's cross-country team won the conference meet five times and only once finished lower than second. The 1980 team won the NCAA western regional. Familiar names in this sport, as well as in track, included Bill Scobey, Danny Grimes, Ken Hammer, Mark Elias, Mark

Conover, Scott Peters, Frank Ebiner, Ramon Morales, Tim Gruber, Cris Romero, and Tony Eddings.

Bud Van Deren's football teams finished second in the Far Western Conference on five occasions. In 1981 they beat major rival UC Davis for the first time since 1969. Stars of the era included Gary Peterson, R.W. Hicks, Mike Bettiga, Richard Spinas, Russ Henschel, Bill Plant, Dean Diaz, Kurt Garl, Eddie Pate, Lance Hunter, Dave Rush, and John Ehlers. Bettiga, Garl, Pate, and Hicks went on to play professional football with the NFL.

But football fell on hard times, with seven losing seasons from 1982-89. Van Deren stepped down as coach after the 1985 season. In 20 years he had coached five conference champions (coach-of-the-year three times). Mike Dolby and his "'Jack Attack" replaced Van Deren. Dolby would last five disappointing seasons.

Men's basketball, after years of cellar dwelling, took a turn for the better in the late 70s. In 1977-78, under coach Jim Cosentino, Humboldt had its first winning record since 1957. The next year they tied for first in the conference and competed in postseason play-offs. Star players included Bruce Fernandez, Carl Massey, Steve Alexander, Daryl Westmoreland, Ray Beer, and Clifford Dyson.

Tom Wood replaced Cosentino as coach in 1981. His teams finished second, third, and tied for first in the NCAC from 1983-85. Named coach of the year in 1983, Wood took his squad to the western regionals. His 1984-85 team boasted the best record in school history, 21-8. His stars included Cliff Dyson, Jeff Fagan, Steve Meredith, Jerry Bush, and Mike Hammond.

(*clockwise*)
Professor Gil Cline conducts jazz *al fresco*; NBC sports commentator Dick Enberg, head of the Parent Fund, 1984-87; wrestling coach Frank Cheek; Alann Steen, HSU journalism professor taken hostage in Beirut in 1987.

The soccer team, coached by Chris Hopper and Alan Exley, placed second once and third twice. Chuck Huntington, Jeff Mittner, Mike Mulligan, Kurt Allen, Mark Asman, Ron La-Graff, Stefan Lepold, and Mike Schneider starred in this sport.

Campus/Community Relations

Though campus / community relations went through their most trying times in the early 70s, by the mid-80s the efforts of President McCrone and people of good will, both on and off campus, had repaired most of the damage.

The president regularly issued reports citing economic and service benefits the community derived from the presence of Humboldt State. In 1975 McCrone and the HSU advisory board raised money for campus projects by sponsoring the first President's Ball at the Eureka Inn. The campus held an open house in 1978. Meanwhile a more elaborate alumni report, *Humboldt Stater,* began publication in 1975, resulting in a rejuvenated alumni association.

President McCrone and local politicians met in a 1980 forum to promote mutual interests. Any cutbacks on campus would also affect the community negatively. More such meetings followed as enrollment and budgets declined.

Fisheries professor George Allen had begun a wastewater aquaculture project in 1971. He reared salmonids in a mixture of treated wastewater and bay water. In 1977 the city of Arcata took over funding of the project and used it to meet the city's wastewater treatment needs. The Arcata Marsh and Wildlife Sanctuary would eventually become a model for environmentally responsible waste disposal.

The community contributed to the university in a number of significant ways. Noted 20s alumnus Monroe Spaght

HSU viewed across Klopp Lake at the Arcata Marsh and Wildlife Sanctuary.

established a distinguished lecture series. A 125-acre land donation expanded Lanphere-Christensen Dunes. The City of Arcata initiated a transit service to benefit students. It also designated four campus buildings as historic sites. The local newspaper donated a typesetting machine to the journalism department. And local retired people, sensitive to the housing shortage, took in student tenants to ease the crunch.

As state budgeting decreased, community members and parents of students responded positively. The Partnership Campaign, initiated in 1983, represented the most comprehensive of these efforts. The campaign raised funds to recruit students and to purchase equipment and instructional materials not provided by the state.

That first Partnership Campaign, chaired by local businesspersons Art Dalianes, Dick Nicholson, and Dale Stanhope, enlisted the help of over 80 volunteers in raising $28,900. (By 1992 the campaign would involve 103 volunteers and raise over $148,000.) Besides the money raised, these annual campaigns produced enrollment increases and closer campus/community relations.

NBC sports commentator Dick Enberg headed another fundraising and recruiting effort, the HSU Parent Fund Drive, begun in 1984. One tangible result of this program was a 25-station computer lab in Founders Hall dubbed the "Friendship Lab."

The future for Humboldt may have looked difficult, but campus and community were a team, determined to face that future together.

CenterArts

CenterArts grew out of The Bridge, which in 1976 began programming lectures and the arts to "bridge" campus and community interests. Arcata already had a thriving live music scene, but The Bridge brought major rock and country performers to Redwood Bowl. In 1980 Peter Pennekamp organized CenterArts in its present form. (The early connection to the University *Center* explains the CenterArts name.)

Since the beginning, artists have enjoyed making the trip to Humboldt. North Coast audiences impress them with the energy they give back to the performers. Artists also appreciate the size of the CenterArts operation:

the chance to get away from the impersonality of professional stagehands and huge presenting organizations.

Humboldt has enjoyed the artists, too — and not just on stage. Current director Sarah Shelley remembers an evening with aboriginal musicians from eight different African tribes. Each tribe insisted on eating and dressing separately from the others. In the cool evening, shortly before the performance, Shelley got an urgent call from an assistant: "Bring some space heaters quick, before they start a fire with the furniture." She remembers, as well, a troupe of Chinese acrobats who wouldn't eat American food. She

found them eviscerating a fish and cooking their evening meal in huge woks on the loading dock of Van Duzer Theatre.

"We've really come off the hill," says Shelley, explaining CenterArts' impact on the community. She points to the local Centro de Información Bilingüe Y Culteral, which grew out of the Chicano Voices festival. Another ethnic festival, Black Visions, led to weekly interfaith multicultural services. And programs for young people, notably Artists in the Schools, will benefit the community for generations to come.

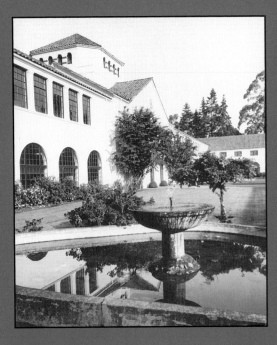

(clockwise from top right) Community Forest bordering campus; New Friendship Macintosh computer lab; tug of war at Lumberjack Days Days,1985; Founders Hall courtyard.

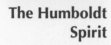

The Humboldt Spirit

excerpts from a 1979 commencement address by Julie Rechtin, printed in Forum

Everyone look out the window. In case your mind has been drifting out there already, don't feel guilty — the redwoods steal the show every year. Take a walk out in the community forest, and you'll see why. The trilliums are turning from white to purple; the salmonberries are turning an edible red; the shrews and mountain beaver are tunneling in the duff; and if you sit awhile, the Douglas fir will start moaning, and the banana slugs will crawl over your shoes.

I've surveyed this forest, tested its soils, keyed out its flora, trapped its rodents, run for hours on its slippery clay trails in the rain, eaten its Himalaya berries — I come out with answers to questions I didn't know I'd asked, humility when I thought my problems were important, strength when I was frustrated. The forest is the kindest teacher by having no sympathy with self-pity, jealousy, or self-importance. . . .

Walk on down to the river, too . . . Stare until you see a spring salmon or a lamprey or a water skimmer. Watch the rocks move; feel the time change. . . .

Walk to the beach. If you stay long enough, the fog will roll in, the dunes will shift, the kites will hover and carry mice into the sky before your eyes. The sea will pound and pound and pound; the waves come in whether any people are there to see them or not . . . Go out to your coast and find out what it has to teach you.

You can go by yourself; you can go with friends or family . . . At Humboldt, I have found a community more cohesive and caring than anyplace I have ever lived. People tell me Arcata does not reflect the real world, that we are sheltered, too much of a utopia, too idealistic — but thank God there are places like this so we realize there are alternatives, that there are places where people know they have the power to change something in their town, be it just a bike bridge over the Mad River, or a clearinghouse on safe energy, or rearing salmon in our sewage.

This is a place where people create their own culture, where we wind Maypoles in the quad, and gather at night to pick and strum our own bluegrass. This is a place where the people have fought big fires all over the West, fished in Alaska, counseled suicide cases, built their own greenhouses, started their own businesses — and they bring it all back to their community. Maybe I was lucky to find a place where I fit in, but I've found lots of other people who say the best friends of their lives have been made in this county.

I think the value of the degree I'm receiving has just as much to do with these friends and this land as it does with this university. I was lucky to find teachers here that recognized that and kept me from holing up in my books — teachers who took me to pulp mills and fault scarps and azalea preserves, teachers who sponsored my journalistic attempts, inspired me to spend hours in the dunes or in city council meetings, laid out running routes through the woods, people who encouraged me to take off quarters to work in the Park Service and travel in the desert — people who realized that school is not a shelter from the world, but a way to keep your mind open while you explore it.

Humboldt's Botanical Bounty

excerpts from an article in *Humboldt Stater* by Sean Kearns

Rooted in tradition, Humboldt State's landscape emphasizes the three R's — redwoods, rhodies, and the rose family — with generous sprays of exotic and common scents. In a cluster of diversity rarely seen beyond the formal botanical gardens, the 160-acre main campus includes representatives of 107 plant families and more than 400 species.

On a slope sandwiched between science buildings A, B, and C stand three redwood species: the dawn of China, the *sempervirens* of the coast, and the *gigantus* of the Sierras. Of the 13 rhododendron species on campus, only two are native to the redwood region. Among the 39 *Rosaceae* members at Humboldt are quince trees, loquat trees, wild strawberry, apple, blackberry, and an evergreen pear. Common scents can be found throughout the grounds.

Humboldt's botanical bounty is apt for a painter's palette. Its swirl holds splashes of scarlet maple, red flowering currant, orange marigolds, yellow honeysuckle, the evergreens of more than 60 conifer species, the "blue gum" eucalyptus, and the perennial purple of huckleberry.

The campus rests in a pocket cut from a swatch of coastal redwoods. Creeks, one a Jolly Giant, thread their way through — and in some parts under — the grounds. Tucked just within the forest is Fern Lake.

According to Humboldt State's grounds supervisor, Wayne Hawkins, "At most campuses, landscaping is just space between buildings, long sweeping lawns and rows of things, a more institutional shape. Humboldt is more the pattern of an ornamental garden, with considerably more diversity, more types of niches."

Humboldt has a tradition of people who place high value on the physical attractiveness of the campus. People like the late Cornelius Siemens, who used to introduce himself as "half-time president, half-time gardener"; President Alistair McCrone, long an advocate of a naturally beautiful, well-maintained Humboldt; Virginia Rumble, former presidential secretary who established a nativeplants garden; professors such as Dennis Walker, who prepared the proverbial bed for an international stand of conifers; former grounds supervisor Lyle Ocheltree, whose visions continue to bloom each spring; and now Hawkins and his crew of seven area gardeners, whose dedication is apparent in everything from dirt to deadwood.

"They must maintain high standards," Hawkins said. "This is not my garden or their garden. It's Humboldt's garden."

The Spirit Continues

1987 - 93

In the years since 1987, Humboldt State has coped with severe budget cuts, increased student fees, continued threats of layoffs, and low morale. On the other hand, academic reorganization, new efforts to recruit and retain students, and better relations between campus and community have helped preserve confidence in the future.

Today Humboldt stands braced for changes in student enrollment, the arrival of new faculty members, new construction projects, and innovative approaches to teaching the liberal arts.

What the pseudonymous Mary Lou Humboldt (p 34) called "this faraway college" remains unique and picturesque. These days, of course, thousands tread where once there were only dozens. The school has lost some of its small-college camaraderie. Still, each incoming student, like Mary Lou, finds this place abounding in possibilities: social, spiritual, and intellectual.

As phrased in the theme of Humboldt State's 75th birthday celebration, "The spirit continues!"

1980s view of Founders Hall from the library.

The university found itself with a new set of problems: insufficient funds, insufficient classes and faculty, and a housing crunch. Admissions issued the following statement:

> After May 1, 1989, Humboldt State University will no longer accept applications from new undergraduate students for the fall, 1989, semester.

Not since the early 70s, when Humboldt was known as "the Cinderella of the North," had the school turned away qualified applicants.

Streamlining & Administrative Moves

Manuel Esteban became the new provost and vice president for academic affairs in 1990. Upon assuming the position, he said, "I want HSU to be the premier CSU campus." He arrived, however, just in time to cope with serious budget questions facing the university.

In 1990, for example, the university found its budget reduced by $2 million. Acting chancellor Ellis McCune characterized that budget as the worst in CSU history, yet in 1991 HSU's budget was cut by another *$7 million*. Cuts over the next two years would go even deeper.

Student fee increases rose steadily and hard-pressed Humboldt administrators eliminated classes, laid off faculty, and limited enrollment even further. Entire departments were cut, including home economics, speech and

Enrollment Ups & Downs

A turning point in enrollment came in 1987. Despite dramatically increasing fees (from $910 in 1988 to $1,308 in 1992), and CSU's higher admission standards (fall of 1988), the student population began to climb. From 1990-93 HSU had even more students than estimated.

**Enrollment Figures
for the Past 10 Years**

	# students	FTEs
82-83	6876	6442
83-84	6285	5896
84-85	6010	5596
85-86	6053	5674
86-87	5843	5290
87-88	6221	5637
88-89	6752	6239
89-90	7301	6741
90-91	7654	7047
91-92	7824	7166
92-93	7851	7326

hearing, and education. President McCrone reduced the vice presidencies from four to three, combining development and administrative affairs under Vice President Don Christensen.

In 1991 HSU streamlined operations by combining colleges to form just four:

> College of Behavioral & Social Sciences
> Lee Bowker, dean
> College of Professional Studies
> Bette Lowery, dean
> College of Arts & Humanities
> Ron Young, dean
> College of Natural Resources & Sciences
> James Smith, dean

Curriculum for teacher training became an all-university responsibility. The two teacher preparation programs, multiple subjects (elementary) and single subjects (secondary), joined the College of Professional Studies.

Not all administrative changes were budget-driven. Brenda Aden became affirmative action officer, and Rena Fowler replaced David Oyler as librarian. Whitney Buck retired in 1993 after 29 years as professor and dean of undergraduate studies. Lily Owyang succeeded him. She came to HSU after a 30-year affiliation with Emmanuel College in Boston. Meanwhile, Manuel Esteban left HSU to become president of CSU, Chico. He was replaced temporarily by "Mr. Interim," John Hennessy, until a permanent successor could be selected.

At the highest level of the CSU system, chancellor Ann Reynolds resigned under fire and Barry Munitz, a businessman with close ties to the Pacific Lumber Company, replaced her in 1991.

Faculty/Staff Transitions

With periodic threats of layoffs, the CSU urged university personnel to reduce their work time, take unpaid leaves, or retire early. Many did retire. Some took advantage of new Golden Handshake plans. Some faculty opted for a plan that allowed them to teach part-time after retirement.

Retirees (and their years of service) included Alwyn Sessions (37); John Russell (36); Henry Tropp (35); Tom Knight and Jack Shaffer (34); Stan Harris (33); James Gast and Richard Ridenhour (32); Barb van Putten (31); Kathryn Corbett and Robert Wallace (30); Frank Jolly, Manuel Kaster, Farris Roy Meredith, and Janet Spinas (27); Alba Gillespie, George Magladry, and John Hennessy (26); Duncan Bazemore (25); Gerald Beck, Jeneral Cranston, Herbert Hendricks, Frank Mahar, Stuart Sundet, and Jack Yarnall (24).

A milestone was passed when Homer Balabanis, "Mr. Humboldt," died in 1991 after a 68-year association with HSU.

With shrinking budgets and little job security, this was another era of pessimism and low faculty morale, particularly when statewide budget cuts threatened the jobs of full-time faculty. President McCrone took action to improve conditions. A task force headed by faculty president Linda Anderson investigated concerns. The president also held small group meetings with faculty and worked with the academic senate in ranking those complaints to be addressed. Where specific grievances received attention (improved clerical support for research, for example, and renovation of classrooms), the resolution led to improved morale.

The McCrone Presidency

In a 1989 interview in *Humboldt Stater* commemorating his first fifteen years as president, Alistair McCrone spoke to how he wanted history to remember his tenure:

> I have no illusions about doing anything other than helping to add to and to release the talents that are already here. I think you have to see your role as part of an enduring institution that will go on without you. If it's just a little bit better than it could have been without you, that's enough.

Three characteristics of McCrone's administrative style set him apart: first, his willingness to delegate responsibilities; second, his strong advocacy of the academic and scholarly aspects of university life; and third, his strong advocacy of the university's image and visibility in the community.

A Reputation for Excellence

Right through the difficult changes of this era, Humboldt maintained its standards of academic excellence. From 1990 to 1992, a *U.S. News and World Report* study ranked Humboldt State among the best universities in the West. This was based on five criteria: 1) quality of the student body, 2) quality of faculty, 3) reputation for academic excellence, 4) financial resources, and 5) ability to recruit and retain graduate students.

Members of the forensics team, Laura Aguada and Mindi Golden, qualified for national competition in St. Louis in 1992. Humboldters placed second at a wildlife conclave in Montana in 1991, with Michele Cardinaux making the outstanding student presentation. On a faculty level, wildlife's Rick Botzler was the CSU's outstanding professor in 1992.

HSU alumni made names for themselves during this era. Robert Detweiler (social science, 1960) became president of CSU, Dominguez Hills in 1989. In 1990 Jeff Self (fisheries, 1971) received a presidential award for teaching excellence in science and math. Bruce Fisher (multiple subjects, 1975) was named California teacher of the year in 1991.

Spotlight on the Arts

The departments of art, music, and theatre arts, traditionally strong on campus, caught the spotlight in the mid-80s.

Pop singer Madonna contributed $700,000 worth of equipment to theatre arts in 1987, the same year the campus hosted the American College Theatre Festival.

Beginning the following summer, Humboldt hosted CSU's Summer Arts festival. (The CSU awarded the festival to Humboldt for an additional three years in 1992.) Summer Arts involves students and faculty from the CSU and elsewhere in short-term performance projects. It also features performances and master classes by accomplished artists. One permanent consequence of Summer Arts' presence was a sculpture, *Humboldt Ship,* built on the south lawn of the Balabanis Complex by guest artist John Roloff.

Meanwhile CenterArts, under directors Peter Pennekamp (1980), Anne Yard (1988), and Sarah Shelley (1989), brought high profile professional performers to campus, from classical and traditional artists to the contemporary and avant-garde.

Stateline, the official publication of the CSU, recognized Humboldt's excellence in the visual and performing arts. So did the National Endowment for the Arts, calling it "a model program in the West." (In 1988 CenterArts director Peter Pennekamp would be lured away by the NEA to direct their InterArts program in Washington, D.C.)

The Generosity of Friends

Humboldt received several major gifts in this era, each contributing further to the university's academic excellence. (Appendix B has a more complete list.)

Industrialist Louis Schatz established an endowment and donated a 385-acre stand of hardwood trees near Maple Creek for forestry research. He also gave $760,000 to endow an innovative research project converting sunlight into hydrogen gas and, through fuel cells, into electricity.

Fortuna native Henry Trione arranged for Wells Fargo Bank to donate an abandoned branch building (valued at $435,000) to house a natural history museum. The Katherine Morningstar Trust gave an additional $150,000 for the bank-to-museum conversion, and $58,000 in grants from the Humboldt Area Foundation went to purchase showcases. The museum bought its 2,000 piece fossil collection (termed "the finest west of the Mississippi") from Hilda and Tom Maloney using $100,000 of private funds and lottery grants. Under the supervision of geology professor John Longshore, the Humboldt State Museum of Natural History opened in May of 1989.

Campus Changes

Talk of a new regional University of California campus titillated local residents for a while, then came to naught. In the meantime the North Coast's existing university campus kept improving. HSU added a new building to house student and business services as well as a new complex of residence halls.

With tight budgets, however, most funds went into remodeling and repair of existing buildings. New elevators aided the handicapped. To aid everyone's breathing, smoking was banned in campus buildings. Founders Hall was vacated for two years, beginning in late 1990, for complete renovation.

The Rathskeller, in the University Center, was remodeled and renamed The Depot. The pool tables and game room moved into the old Corner Deli area, replaced by Associated Students offices, meeting rooms, and a study area. Food service and bookstore areas also underwent remodeling in the summers of 1991 and 1992.

Construction began in 1989 on a student and business services building at the south end of the Gist Hall parking lot. To compensate for the loss of parking, a new lot was built south of Griffith Hall, and other lots were expanded. In November, 1990, most of the offices housed in the university annex (the old Trinity Hospital) moved into the new building. So did financial aid, the testing center, extended education, graphics, and public safety.

In the fall of 1992, students occupied four new residence halls — Creekview Apartments, in the Jolly Giant Creek area. Accommodating 252 students in groups of five, Creekview offered kitchens, living rooms, lounges, fireplaces, and other amenities.

The Giving Tradition

The $12,000 Arcata residents pledged to start the school, plus William Preston's gift of land for a campus, began a tradition of private support that has nurtured Humboldt State for eight decades. Today, according to development director Jan Petranek, more than 4,000 alumni and friends support the school.

From 1983-93 alumni, parents, foundations, corporations, and the local community raised their annual giving from $175,000 to $1.5 million. Tangible results of this support appear throughout the campus: library collections, microcomputer laboratories, art collections, specially-equipped teaching rooms, scientific equipment, numerous scholarships, and several distinguished lecture series.

Academic Matters

For much of the 80s, the more popular majors were business, computer information systems, environmental engineering, geology, and the natural resources. This trend reflected the more job-conscious student population. By the early 90s, however, the humanities, social sciences, and visual and performing arts were on the rise. In part, this reflected increasing nationwide demand for public school teachers. Teacher credential programs attracted the most majors in the early 90s.

Natural History Museum in Wells Fargo Hall, 1989; Schatz Solar Hydrogen Project at the marine lab in Trinidad.

The sundial in front of the library was donated by Harry S. Kieval, emeritus professor of mathematics; Colleen Mullery, assistant professor of business administration, with a student in a computer lab.

Natural resources experienced dramatic declines in the late 80s. By 1991 employment in these areas was grim, reflecting a Reagan-era decline in spending by governmental agencies. Eventually even the number of business majors declined.

New programs on campus included a major in computer information systems, a biochemistry and toxicology emphasis, a religious studies major, and dramatic writing and directing emphases in theatre arts. Chancellor Munitz also made Humboldt a center for resolution of environmental disputes. As a result, by 1992 HSU offered a major in environmental studies, combining ethics and technology.

With the 90s came a drive to make the curriculum more multicultural. In keeping with a national trend, the university adopted a three-year program initiated by ITEPP director Lois Risling. HSU encouraged departments in the social sciences and humanities to promote knowledge of, and appreciation for, the nation's cultural diversity. Cultural Diversity Week, begun in 1991, further celebrated this. Samuel Betances, a popular speaker on multiculturalism, visited campus in 1992.

Campus Life

In 1990 British filmmakers built cultural bridges through *Humboldt-Humboldt,* a film comparing and contrasting student life at HSU and Humboldt-Universität in East Berlin, Germany. They found a reasonably contented student body among the California Humboldters. A 1990 survey revealed that HSU students liked their institution better than the students of any other CSU campus (though they rated food service lowest of the 18 campuses surveyed).

Skateboarding and bicycling regained popularity. The Par Infinity Club devised flying disc golf, creating an 18-hole course in the woods behind the tennis courts.

Greeks continued their comeback. By 1992 HSU had seven fraternities and sororities, all trying to shun the Animal House image of yesteryear. Lumberjack Days organizers, too, responded to community complaints over noise and

drinking. In 1989 they began deemphasizing alcohol consumption.

Again in this era, a number of celebrities visited campus: jazz musicians "Dizzy" Gillespie, Wynton Marsalis, and Herbie Mann; U.S. Senator Alan Cranston; actress Nina Foch; satirist Mark Russell; sports commentator Dick Enberg; Native American flutist Carlos Nakai; and musician Taj Mahal, to name a few. Another "visit," a rare four-inch snowfall, closed the campus in February of 1989.

Unfortunately, there were bad times too. In 1988 the campus was stunned by news that graduate student Danielle Plumb Zumbrum had been murdered while jogging in the Arcata Community Forest. While the body of her suspected killer was later found, the incident aroused much fear and anger on campus. Safety patrols organized, and Students Against Violent Events (SAVE) promoted safety on campus.

Student Attitudes

At every commencement ceremony since 1987, HSU graduates have been asked to pledge

> to investigate thoroughly and take into account the social and environmental consequences of any job opportunities I consider.

Known for its socially conscious student body, HSU continued to rank high among universities in the number of Peace Corps volunteers (37 overseas in 1989). Social and political concerns of the late 80s and early 90s, as expressed in *The Lumberjack*, were abortion, recycling, AIDS, rape, sexual harassment, campus crime, and the environment. The campus observed the 20th anniversary of Earth Day. Cultural Diversity Week lifted up the ideals of multiculturalism. The American Sign Language Club held Silent Sunday to address the needs of persons with speaking disabilities.

Youth Educational Services reached out to the Humboldt County jail and assisted teenage mothers through a family issues program. A new Adult Re-entry Center helped older students make the transition to college life.

Professor Ken Lang's biology class at Clam Beach, 1992; Lourin Plant, assistant professor of music, conducts a vocal ensemble.

Track star Denise Walker in 1990 cross-country championships; student field trip on HSU's research vessel equipped to do biological, physical, geological and chemical sampling.

Native American Programs

Since the late 60s, Humboldt State has fostered several highly successful programs in support of the local Native American communities. Besides the CICD (see p 96) two of the most prominent are ITEPP and NACENR.

The Indian Teacher Education Project began in 1969 as an effort to make institutional changes in the public school system. ITEP would train qualified American Indian educators who could teach "the necessities of life" in the dominant society without sacrificing tribal identity.

ITEP became the Indian Teacher and Educational Personnel Program in 1979, when it expanded to include ancillary educational personnel such as school counselors, psychologists and social workers. Now the oldest and most successful program in the nation, it remains active in recruitment, orientation, financial aid and academic advising, advocacy, job placement and more.

Native American Career Education in Natural Resources — now called INRSEP (Indian Natural Resource, Science, & Engineering Program) — was established in 1974. The program uses counseling and curriculum support services to increase Indian and Alaska native students' chances for success in science and natural resource disciplines.

Students have been placed in cooperative education assignments with the U.S. Forest Service and the Fish & Wildlife Service, as well as in private industry.

Student Government

Student government became more active in this era. The SLC's Otis Johnson became a liaison to the Arcata city council. Associated Students established a commissioner for external affairs as a permanent liaison with the off-campus community.

Former ASB president Bill Crocker served a student term on the CSU board of trustees. ASB also rejoined the state associated students organization. In 1988-89, Humboldt's Allison Weber became the first woman to chair the organization. The next year, Vicki Allen served on it as well.

Associated Students and the University Center occasionally clashed. Sponsorship of certain activities overlapped (intramurals, CenterArts). Associated Students wanted more say in running the University Center and Lumberjack Enterprises. In 1990 the SLC transferred management responsibility for the AS business office to the University Center's general manager, Joan Tyson. Students also accepted a new AS constitution, streamlining student government by eliminating unnecessary committees and procedures.

An interesting election in 1990 pitted so-called Progressive candidates against Greeks (the fraternity/sorority contingent). Progressives won, with Randy Villa becoming AS president. That election also included a Better Food Initiative, calling for expanded menus and healthier foods from Lumberjack Enterprises. It carried by a smashing 9-1 vote.

During 1991 and 1992, students sent representatives to Sacramento to protest fee hikes, to protest the war against Iraq, and to support cultural diversity and a multicultural curriculum.

Athletic Reorganization

In 1989, after a four-year hiatus, cheerleading crews — megaphones, pompoms, and all — returned to the home football and basketball games. Vern Hendricks organized the first eight members: Darlene Argentini, Valerie Buss, Kellie Coureen, Michelle Dolby, Vesna Grubic, Raylene McDowell, Rebecca Melvin, and Anne Rusiewicz. Mean-while the Marching Lumberjacks continued to exhibit their special brand of craziness.

As described below, some of the athletic teams experienced remarkable success. Still, as in so many other areas of the university, athletics had to confront budgetary concerns. Wrestling and swimming were dropped. Fundraising took up a greater portion of the total effort. Keeping the Northern California Athletic Conference together posed yet another problem. Sacramento State and Notre Dame dropped out, and many feared UC Davis might soon bolt to NCAA division I, leaving the conference leaner and posing significant scheduling problems.

Men's Athletics

In 1989-90 coach Tom Wood's basketball team tied UC Davis for first, then won the NCAC postseason tournament over San Francisco State. Wood was named western regional coach of the year. Several "building years" followed that season. Star players of this era included Ron Connors, Sandy Johnson, Eddie Whitmore, Alan Erickson, Mike Figert, Jack Bainbridge, and Stan Twitchell.

In wrestling, Frank Cheek became the NCAC's and HSU's most victorious coach. Star wrestlers included Robert Watkins, Tim Monohan, Mike Puzz, and Dean Henderson. Heavyweight Luke Parham won the national title in 1990. Unfortunately, due to budget considerations and several conference members dropping the sport, HSU dropped intercollegiate wrestling.

Dave Wells' cross-country teams won conference championships in 1988, 1990, 1991, and 1992. The 1991 team finished third in the division II national championships. Wells was named both conference and western regional coach of the year. His star runners included Mike Jekabsons, Bill Schipper, Bill Frampton, Chris Hobson, Peter Oviatt, Chris Mullaney, and Chris Parmer.

While Wells did not win the conference title in track and field, he did coach some outstanding long-distance runners. James Williams became sprint coach beginning with the Olympic Festival in the summer of 1991. Track stars included Craig Olson, Dennie Pfeifer, Reed Elmore, Rodney Dickerson, Jim Bowles, and James Olson.

Coach Alan Exley's 1989 soccer team had an impressive 15-6 record. It featured Ken Sintchak and Kevin Wiese, both on the all-western regional team. Exley was named Far West coach of the year for NCAA division II. Other star players during the era were Todd Keough, Randy Kidd, Scott Power, Mike Taft, and Kamika Sherwood.

Fred Whitmire, an HSU hall-of-fame athlete and former College of the Redwoods football coach, replaced Mike Dolby in 1991. In his first two seasons, the Lumberjacks had a combined 13-9 record. Star football players under the two head coaches included Pat Johnson, Corny Ross, Dave Booth, Rodney Dorsett, Richard Ashe, Dave Harper, Scott Reagan, Freeman Baysinger, and Dave Tullar.

Women's Athletics

Wendy Becker, selected division II all-American for her 10,000 meter performance in 1988, became Humboldt's first nationally recognized track star since Elta Cartwright in 1928. Other star runners on coach Dave Wells' teams included Lisa Harper, Kimbra Macauley, Denise Walker, and Juan Ball. The cross-country teams were competitive also. Wendy Becker was a champion again. Track star Denise Walker also won cross-country all-American honors at the 1990 national meet. Summer Ecberg lead the team in 1992.

Women's basketball fought for respectability under coach Pam Martin. The 1988-89 squad placed third in the conference and played the first postseason game for Humboldt women. They reached postseason play again in 1992. Among the stars were Dawn Miner, Janay Bainbridge, conference player of the year Carrie LaBudde, and division II all-American Suzie Farmer.

After struggling for several years, the volleyball team, under Janis Rowe-Grondalski, placed second in the NCAC in 1988.

Alumnus Mark Conover wins '88 Olympic marathon trials.

Dan Collen and Julie Ortman took over the coaching the next year. They honed the talents of stars such as Abby Ackroyd, Shauna Dada, Angela Erken, and Teresa Walters.

Swim teams, first under coach Pam Armold, then Sue Rodearmel, struggled against strong competition. In 1990, however, the team boasted its best finish in 12 years (third), and Rodearmel was named NCAC coach of the year. (Not enough, apparently, as the sport became one of HSU's budget cuts.) Outstanding individual swimmers included Lyn Brock, Kari Irvin, Sue Pettit, Melissa Benson, and divers Kirsten Keithly and Shannon Speier.

When softball returned after a six-year absence, coach Frank Cheek led his team to conference championships in 1989, 1990, 1991, and 1993. The latter placed third in the Western regionals. These teams featured all-Americans Cheryl Clark and Jeri Hildebrand. Other stars included Becky Immel, Cristi Hulse, and Teresa Cheek (pitcher of the year in the NCAC). Standout pitchers Torrie Cababa and Sue Ellen Stallard led the 1991 team to a 39-10 record.

Town & Gown Partnership

Several emotionally charged events caused friction between campus and community. Timber industry spokespersons complained of a lack of support from the campus. They took exception to research on the endangered spotted owl.

A parking controversy emerged in 1989. The CSU raised parking fees at the same time Humboldt reduced parking space behind Gist Hall to make room for the student and business services building. When students parked in residential areas near the campus, residents complained. A three-pronged approach helped remedy the situation:

1) residents received permits and preference for parking in front of their homes, while parking in other areas was restricted to two or four hours;

Earthquake Information

sources:
The Lumberjack
(various years);
On Shaky Ground,
by Lori Dengler
and Kathy Moley

Since the late 40s, Humboldt State has had seismographic reporting stations on campus. In 1962, amid much local publicity, a new instrument was set up in the basement of Nelson Hall to measure surface waves in the earth's crust.

Today, using ever more sophisticated equipment, HSU continues to serve the region with its earthquake research. Earthquake safety booklets, like the recent *On Shaky Ground,* prepare the community for the next "big one."

Historically, the North Coast accounts for about one quarter of all earthquake energy released in California. The Gorda (tectonic) Plate subducts beneath the North American Plate all along the coast; and at Cape Mendocino, the additional abutment of the Pacific Plate creates a dangerous triple junction. Slippage along the resulting faults resulted in some strong North Coast earthquakes (greater than magnitude 5.5) in 1906, 1922, 1923, 1932, 1954, and 1980. More than 60 quakes have caused damage since 1850. The area shook to magnitude 7.1, 6.6, and 6.7 quakes in April, 1992.

John C. Young, geology professor, works on the visual recorder of the HSC seismograph station in 1971, with Roy Kohl, geology department technician.

2) to encourage students to ride the bus, the Arcata city council matched HSU subsidies to the Arcata-Mad River Transit System; and

3) to promote safer bicycling to and from campus, Arcata established bike lanes on L.K. Wood Boulevard.

Another controversy loomed in January, 1991, when the city council established Arcata as a sanctuary for opponents to the Persian Gulf War. The issue proved quite divisive, and some who opposed the council's move associated the university with the antiwar sentiments. Later it became clear that individuals from *both* town and gown could be numbered among the supporters and denouncers of the resolution.

But positive campus/community relations developed as well. Wells Fargo Bank, as mentioned earlier, donated its Arcata branch building to HSU for use as a museum of natural history.

The university linked up with Native American communities with the appointment of Victor Golla to the Center for Community Development. In 1989 students carved redwood canoes in the Yurok tradition under the tutelage of artist-in-residence George Blake of Hoopa. One canoe remains on display in the library.

The Humboldt Chorale, a joint student/community venture founded by Lee Barlow in 1947, grew to more than 130 members under the energetic direction of Ken Hannaford.

"Happy Birthday to You"

"The Spirit Continues" was the theme for HSU's 75th anniversary observance in 1988-89. An open house, a special homecoming celebration, a golf tournament, an Alexander von Humboldt exhibit, and other events celebrated the university's past, present, and future.

Stressing cooperation and community, President McCrone asked members of the campus community to strive to make Humboldt State University a place where the idea of leaving the world in a condition worthy of the privilege of life itself is both inspiration and commitment . . . May what we today call the "Humboldt Spirit" always be with you.

The Future

Faced with a potential student enrollment explosion in the 90s, the university braces itself for change. HSU finds itself in the unusual position of having to lay off faculty and staff while the number of students is on the rise. This presents a dilemma which may require changes in the state and national economy, particularly in the tax base for higher education.

The university has begun considering a proposal by Chancellor Munitz that would make Humboldt a "charter" campus. Charter status would exempt the school from certain restrictive bureauratic measures and encourage experimentation and innovation in curriculum, teaching methods, funding, and management.

Meanwhile President McCrone has appointed a commission on future directions and missions to take stock of the university's situation and recommend goals. The president outlined his own vision for the future in his 1989 State-of-the-University address:

1) an enhanced emphasis on teaching
2) maintenance of the liberal arts tradition
3) support for scholarship, especially that involving students
4) good faculty/student relations
5) mutual trust and respect between faculty and administrators
6) a humanistic environment
7) a return to reading classics as well as current literature

If this is the Humboldt Spirit, then may that spirit continue.

(clockwise from top right) Sue Lee, professor of biology, (second from right) with members of WINS —Women in Natural Resources and Sciences; commencement in Redwood Bowl; Student and Business Services Building; students at HSU's observatory on Fickle Hill, 1990.

133

Appendix A

Humboldt State Chronology

1912

Dec   Senator William Kehoe and Assemblyman Hans Nelson introduce legislation to establish a normal school in Humboldt County

1913

Jun   (13th) Governor Hiram Johnson signs law establishing a "Humboldt State Normal School" to train elementary school teachers

Sep   Governor appoints board of trustees: five local members, governor and state superintendent of instruction *ex officio* members

Nov   (13th) HSNS trustees select Arcata as location for the normal school • (19th) state attorney general declares actions of trustees null and void

1914

Jan   Board of trustees names Nelson Van Matré president of HSNS

Feb   (14th) HSNS trustees, meeting in Sacramento, reaffirm decision to locate normal in Arcata

Apr   (6th) Humboldt State Normal School begins in Arcata Grammar School, 11th and L streets • 78 students and 5 faculty by May 1

Fall   William Preston and Union Water Co. stockholders donate 51 acres east of Arcata for permanent site of HSNS

Dec   First play performed, *Her Own Way*

1915

May   First graduation, in Minor Theatre: 15 women; first grad is Susie Baker Fountain

Jun   Construction of temporary building on the "Preston Tract"

Fall   Horace "Pop" Jenkins joins faculty

1916

Jan   HSNS moves into temporary building (present site of Founders Hall) • 156 students

Student loan fund established by community

1917

Apr   (6th) U.S. enters World War I

Jun   Legislature appropriates funds to build new administration building (now Founders Hall)

1920

Swimming pool built in the gulch behind temporary building

1921

Jun   (1st) HSNS renamed Humboldt State Teachers College and Junior College • (28th) HSNS trustees dissolved • department of education (Sacramento) designated authority over college

Administration building completed

1923

Fall   Homer Balabanis joins faculty

1924

Sum   Ralph Swetman becomes new president

Fall   Associated Student Body organized (Howard Trueblood first president) • alumni association formed (Hugh Stewart first president) • first homecoming • first student newspaper, *The Foghorn* • comedy performed by students and faculty, *The College Jinx*

1925

Fall   Laura Herron joins faculty and organizes Women's Athletic Association

Play Day and Work Day initiated

1927

Humboldt State authorized to offer B.A.

Spr   First yearbook, *Cabrillo*

Fall   First intercollegiate football contest: loss to Southern Oregon Normal, 33-0 (coach Fred Telonicher)

1928

Spr Humboldt State Teachers College Improvement Foundation established

Sum "Cinder" Elta Cartwright, Humboldt track star, participates in first U.S. women's Olympic team in Amsterdam

1929

Oct Stock market crash on Wall Street

Fall New student newspaper published, HSTC *Rooter*

1930

Sum Ralph Swetman leaves Humboldt • Arthur Gist becomes new president

Fall HSTC *Rooter* renamed *The Lumberjack*

Chi Sigma Epsilon honor society formed, J. Wendell Howe sponsor

1931

Spr New gymnasium completed and dedicated • first high school senior day on campus

1932

Fall Enrollment reaches 388 • teacher placement bureau established • Little Symphony Orchestra, A Cappella Choir, pep band formed • tuition goes from $1.50 to $6.50 per semester • HSTC offers A.B. degree in biology, English, social sciences, and kindergarten — primary education

1933

Sum California Department of Education threatens to close HSTC

Fall College Elementary School completed (Gist Hall)

Alumni association publishes *Humboldt Alumnus,* edited by Alta McElwain and J. Wendell Howe

1934

Apr Humboldt celebrates 20th anniversary

Spr Civil Works Administration provides fund to improve buildings and grounds • first intercollegiate tennis team (coach Monica Wright)

1935

Fall HSTC renamed Humboldt State College • 275 students, 31 faculty • Football coach Charles Erb has 6-1-1 record for Thunderbolts

1936

Spr First intercollegiate track meet, losing to Chico State 103-26

Fall Football star Vernon Thornton is "champion doughnut eater" after eating 24 of Pop Jenkins' doughnuts in one sitting • sports mascot changed to Lumberjacks

1937

Fall Student-run "cooperative bookstore and fountain" opens • HSC offers B.S. in education

1938

Fall Forestry Club organized

1939

Spr Legislature appropriates fund to build new dormitory (now Nelson Hall) and playground for College Elementary School

Fall Library acquires copy of Hitler's *Mein Kampf*

Sep World War II begins • Associated Women Students organized

1940

Fall Men's sports join Far Western Conference • William and Hortense Lanphere begin two-year wildlife management program • ski club builds lodge on Horse Mountain • first annual pancake feed for faculty and students at Camp Bauer • aeronautics class trains pilots • faculty council organized by the state colleges

1941

Fall Queen of the Campus sponsored by Mutsuhito Club (name changed to Favonians after Dec 7) • enrollment high of 481 students • Gist bans hazing of freshmen • radio training offered for women

Oct HSC Radio Workshop aired on KIEM

1942

Spr Air observation post built atop college commons • Skywatch near Redwood Park, operated by faculty wives • *The War Effort* variety show

Fall Football abolished • commando physical fitness offered by phys ed department • President Gist initiates *Humboldt News Letter* to send to men and women in the armed services

1943

Fall   *With the Armed Forces* column featured in *Lumberjack* • Humboldt Hilarities proceeds go for war bonds and Red Cross

1944

Spr   23 men, 4 women graduate • main building (now Founders Hall) camouflaged

Fall   Enrollment drops to 176

1945

Fall   HSC organized into five divisions • Homer Balabanis dean of arts • Harry Griffith dean of education • Charles Fulkerson reorganizes HSC Symphony, includes community participation

1946

Fall   HSC accredited by NW Association of Secondary and Higher Schools • new faculty include Leland Barlow, Kate Buchanan, Reese Bullen, Joseph Forbes, William Jackson, Hyman Palais, Roscoe Peithman • Humboldt Village and Redwood Hall house married students and veterans • students and community build bleachers for Redwood Bowl • new clubs include Knights, Wildlife, Student Federalists

1947

Spr   Far Western Conference reactivated

Fall   Speech/radio major offered • radio station KHSC established • enrollment reaches 750 • G.I. Wives and Rally Committee established • first graduate classes offered (History of Economic Thought; U.S. Colonial History) • Sweetheart and Harvest balls held • NW California Dramatics Festival for high school students • B.A. in wildlife management established • lights installed in Redwood Bowl

1948

Mar   California Department of Education establishes HSC enrollment capacity at 1,418 students

Spr   World War II camouflaging of main building finally painted over

Fall   HSC advisory council established — administrators, faculty, and students

1949

Fall   HSC offers general secondary teaching credential, 18 B.A. degrees, five B.S. degrees

Oct   President Gist suffers heart attack • Homer Balabanis is interim president

1950

May   Industrial arts building, Jenkins Hall, completed • state funding surpasses $500,000 • All-College Picnic held at Camp Bauer

Jun   President Gist retires • Korean War begins

Jul   Cornelius Siemens named president

Fall   Siemens appoints HSC advisory board

Oct   *Conservation Unlimited* published • M.A. degree in teaching of drama, education, and social science

Nov   Greater Humboldt Committee formed

1951

Apr   New Coop built

Sep   Jessie T. Woodcock retires after 31 years

Fall   Two-year programs established in dairying and lumbering and logging • marching band formed

Dec   Conservation Week held

1952

Spr   HSC Foundation established • Coop has coffee for 7¢, hamburger 25¢

Sep   Library dedicated (now Van Matré Hall) • Peace Carillon dedicated • new faculty: Dan Brant, John Pauley, Charles Bloom, Kathryn Corbett • science building and corporation yard finished

Fall   Football team, coached by Phil Sarboe, wins FWC for first time

1953

Spr   Chas. Barnum endows local history contest

Mar   Bunny Hop held in Eureka

Sep   Skywatch ended • Frosh Camp orients new students • 26 new faculty include Milt Dobkin and Leon Wagner • "Pop" Jenkins dies

Oct   Wildlife management building finished

Dec   Christmas flood

1954

Feb   Faculty members Charles Parke, Ralph Roske, and Dan Brant are candidates for Muddy Gras king

Spr   Maurice Hicklin and Homer Arnold retire after more than 30 years • Adlai Stevenson attends All-College Picnic • west stands in Redwood Bowl covered with roof

1955

Fall   Football star Earl Meneweather installed as first member of HSC Sports Hall of Fame

1956

Fall   Division of Natural Resources established • 89 courses of study offered (41 in 1946)

1957

Spr Myrtle McKittrick retires as registrar and placement officer • *Hilltopper* first issued

Fall New buildings include art-home economics, music, men's gym, home management cottage, outdoor facilities for wildlife management • Delta Sigma Phi organized • enrollment at 1527 • Green and Gold Room opened

1958

Spr IBM punch cards used for registration and recording of grades • Tau Kappa Epsilon organized • College Cove is popular sunbathing area

Mar Marriage Education Week observed

May Ground broken for two new dormitories: Redwood and Sunset halls • faculty and staff hold first salmon bake

Sep Enrollment 1921 • 36 new faculty (total 156)

Oct Hula Hoop contest held in Redwood Hall • chartered flight takes team and fans to football game vs. Hawaii

1959

Feb NDEA loans available • indoor swimming pool completed

May Track and field wins its first FWC championship (coach Robert Doornik) • Delta Zeta organized • Lumberjack Days replace All-College Picnic as spring event • B.S. in nursing and A.B. in industrial arts • 45th commencement is largest ever, 225 grads

Fall Student Counseling Center operates in dean of students' offices • parking fees ($13 per semester) instituted for first time • 41 new faculty hired • first issue of *Annual Ring,* Forestry Club publication • new

administration building (now Siemens Hall) • new language arts building and field house • Sunset and Redwood halls occupied • Lucky Logger adopted as mascot • Elta "Cinder Elta" Cartwright is first woman in HSC Sports Hall of Fame

Nov Main building (old administration building) renamed Founders Hall

1960

Jan M.A. in biology approved

Mar HSC chapter of Association of Cal State College Professors formed

Apr California master plan for higher education

Spr All-weather track installed in Redwood Bowl • alumni association begins Who's Who award to distinguished alums (first, George Hogan, '33)

May Sequoia Theatre (now Van Duzer) dedicated • new health center and cafeteria

Sep Per master plan, authority for 14 colleges of CSC system transferred to separate board of trustees; first chancellor, Dr. Buell Gallagher • new divisions established for biological and physical sciences • new coop opens, now called student activities center • enrollment over 2,000

Oct Lumberjack Enterprises established for vending and food services, bookstore, etc. • football games played in Albee Stadium, as Redwood Bowl too small for the crowds

Dec HSC championship team plays Lenoir-Rhyne in NAIA's Holiday Bowl

1961

Feb Enrollment fees now $43 per semester • academic senate meets for first time • Associated Women Students sponsor Women's Day • ASB presidents of CSC system

form CSC Student Presidents' Association • Fred Telonicher elected first general faculty president

May Ugly Professor contest held • Imogene Platt retires after 35 years • recruiting for Peace Corps begins • tennis courts built south of field house

Mashed Potato Incident

Fall HSC has 59 degree-granting programs: 39 BA/BS, 20 MA/MS

Dec Sale of *Tropic of Cancer* banned in county

1962

Jan Metro Bus Service of Arcata operates from post office to campus

Mar CSC trustees predict HSC will have 12,000 students by 1990

Fall Forestry building and new library completed • old library (now Van Matré Hall) remodeled for engineering • enrollment record, 2398 • 30 new faculty • civil defense seeks adequate fallout shelters on campus • legislature initiates Outstanding Teacher award • CSC and academic senate initiate Outstanding Professor award • HSC terminates junior college program

Oct Cuban Missile Crisis

1963

Mar Faculty elects reappointment and tenure committee and promotion committee

May Outstanding Alumnus Monroe Spaght delivers commemorative speech for 50th anniversary • Chancellor Dumke encourages statewide academic senate • end of baccalaureate services

Fall Enrollment reaches 2,628 • 25 new faculty hired • education/psychology building completed (now Harry Griffith Hall)

Nov President John F. Kennedy assassinated

1964

Feb Humboldt County Junior College District establishes College of the Redwoods

Mar New ASB constitution • Barry Goldwater visits to campaign for presidency

Apr Homer Balabanis, first vice president for academic affairs, retires after 40 years, replaced by interim VP Ivan Milhous • Golden Anniversary of HSC observed

Fall Enrollment reaches 2,893; 34 new faculty

Oct Ronald Reagan visits

Dec-Jan Humboldt/Del Norte flood isolates campus; gym facilities used for community relief efforts

1965

Jan College of the Redwoods begins operation in Eureka High School

Feb *Pacific Oceanic Olio* first published

Mar Federal Economic Opportunity Act of 1964 provides money for work-study programs

Sep James Turner is vice president for academic affairs • enrollment 3,100 • 55 new faculty

Fall HSC adopts master plan for future campus development • Arcata requests 5,000 FTE limit on students • Fred Telonicher and Harry Griffith become first Outstanding Professor awardees

Oct Chapter of SNCC, Student Nonviolent Coordinating Committee, founded

Dec Speakers Stump established on commons • Vietnam committee established

1966

Jan Harry Griffith dies after 27 years at HSC • student athletic committee established

Feb First Clam Beach Run

Mar Students agree to build new student union

Spr Marine laboratory opens in Trinidad • William Lanphere retires after 30 years • last issue, for now, of *Sempervirens*

May First graduation held in Redwood Bowl

Sum Upward Bound program begins

Fall 250 faculty, 3,600+ students • auto-mechanics building completed • ACSCP campaigning for collective bargaining • John Gimbel named Outstanding Professor for CSC system • Center for Community Development established, Bill Murison director • Frank "Bud" Van Deren new head football coach

1967

Feb Experimental College organized with 100 students • Vietnam seminar held • first Intercollegiate Kite Flying Contest held at Clam Beach

May Retirees include Helen Everett, Ivan Milhous, Fred Telonicher

Fall Change to quarter system • 3,891 students • "teach-in" on the draft held • College of the Redwoods moves south of Eureka

1968

Jan First registration by computer

Apr Carroll Hurd hired as new vice president of academic affairs

Spr First Film Festival • retirement of Kate Buchanan and John Van Duzer

Fall Donald Strahan becomes first dean for administrative affairs • Jolly Giant Commons and eight dormitories completed • Marching Lumberjacks return after 10-year absence • 72 new faculty, 4,604 students • football team wins FWC; defeats Fresno in Camellia Bowl (coach Bud Van Deren)

Dec Lady Bird Johnson dedicates Redwood National Park • Bill Johnson, chief of plant operations, retires after 27 years

1969

Jan HSC chapter of Sierra Club organized • art and music buildings completed

Feb Freeway issue heats up • ASB establishes student judiciary

Apr Peer group concept adopted for dorm living • trustees approve new student union • President Siemens approves seating students on 37 campus committees • mini-skirt contest held

May Women's track wins Women's Recreation Association meet • Humboldt Honeys started

Fall 5,100 students • academic reorganization: five schools plus division of Health and PE; Milt Dobkin vice president for academic affairs; Whitney Buck dean for undergraduate studies; Richard Ridenhour dean for academic planning; Donald Strahan vice president for administrative affairs; Thomas Stipek first ombudsman • ITEPP begins • co-ed dorms • Vietnam Moratorium Day on Arcata Plaza

1970

Jan *Lumberjack's* Mike Stockstill declares Joe College dead • environmental symposium

Spr Third World Coalition promotes interests of minority students • HOP replaces Frosh Week for new student orientation

May	Protest of Cambodian incursion • Kent State shooting and bombings across nation • vote on Sequoia Quad for voluntary, peaceful, one-week strike • Governor Reagan orders all CSC campuses closed

Jul	College Elementary School closed for remodeling

Sep	Cluster College pilot program initiated after Smith River Retreat • 10,000 apply for admission, only 1,600 accepted • enrollment at 5,479, with 50 new faculty • *R.V. Catalyst* is new oceanography vessel • Ryan Bill creates multiple- and single-subjects credentials

Fall	SLC votes to do away with homecoming queen • YES has 12 outreach programs

1971

Jan	Biology complex completed • United Native Americans organized

Feb	State master plan predicts 10,000 FTE by 1980

Spr	Earl Meneweather appointed ombudsman: first African American administrator

Fall	Student services reorganized: Karshner retires and Thomas MacFarlane is dean • students 18 and over may now register to vote • meal prices: breakfast $1.10, lunch $1.40, dinner $1.65, full day $2.40

Oct	Kerr Tower opened for meditation

1972

Feb	Campus organizations include MEChA, UNA, and HSU Caucus for Women • expansion of Highway 101 to four lanes creates controversy

Apr	HSC adopts affirmative action plan • old CES formally renamed Arthur Gist Hall • controversy over Woodlands Proposal for student housing on 86 acres NE of campus

Jun	HSC renamed California State University, Humboldt

Fall	Natural resources building completed • change from civil engineering to environmental engineering • first female Marching Lumberjack

Oct	Humboldt Students for the Reform of Marijuana Laws organizes

Nov	University Center completed

1973

Jan	End of Selective Service • ethnic studies begin • peace march to protest continued involvement in Vietnam

Spr	First issue of *Humboldt Journal of Social Relations* • university leases former Trinity Hospital for administrative offices • Watergate controversy

Sep	President Siemens retires; Milt Dobkin appointed interim president; John Pauley interim vice president for academic affairs • Cypress Hall completed • Delta Sigma Phi dissolves

Oct	President's house sold at auction for $60

Fall	358 faculty: 63 women and 295 men • Forbes Complex completed • CSUH Women's Association formed; Women's Center displaces Faculty Club in former Balabanis House

1974

Jan	Forbes Complex dedicated; includes Women's Gym • new upper division emphasis phase for general education • faculty organizations (except UPC) merge to form Congress on Faculty Associations to promote collective bargaining

Feb	Applications down • Frank Devery retires as business manager after 23 years • gasoline shortage affects student/faculty travel

Apr	Federal law (Title IX) mandates more funding for women's athletics

May	Black Culture Week and Asian-American Awareness Week • Gay People's Union formed • campus chimes heard hourly • HEW funds Native American Career Education in Natural Resources

Jul	Alistair McCrone becomes president

Fall	School renamed Humboldt State University • Sequoia Theatre renamed John Van Duzer Theatre (dedicated in Feb) • enrollment tops 7,500 (6,700 FTE) • women's sports join Northern California Intercollegiate Conference • "Buzz" Webb named dean for student services • cross-country team wins Far Western Conference (Jim Hunt coaches)

1975

Jan	SLC subsidizes Arcata-Mad River Transit and Humboldt Transit Authority in return for lower student bus fares (10¢)

Feb	First annual President's Ball at Eureka Inn

Spr	Alumni publication renamed *Humboldt Stater* • classless Fridays eliminated to economize

Apr	Women's Awareness Week • Ced Kinzer retires • Intercollegiate Knights, campus service organization, ends after 25 years

May	Cinco de Mayo celebrated • Salmon Bake at Camp Bauer for faculty and staff

Jun	Six separate commencements held, one for each school and division of HPE

Fall	Jewish Student Union formed

1976

Feb *Lumberjack* endorsing candidates (anonymously) for local elections, a violation of Title V of the Administrative Code

Mar Native Americans protest celebration of bicentennial of the American Revolution

Apr Battle over building the G-O road through Native American burial grounds • Earth Week celebrated • enrollment crunch and threats of faculty layoffs lead to orderly layoff procedures

Jun Ronald Reagan Redwood Memorial Grove dedicated near 101 off ramp to 14th street

Fall Enlarged health center opens • EOP offers financial and tutoring services

Sep Swine flu epidemic hits campus

Oct TKE dissolves • new chapter of National Organization of Women • branch of Humboldt National Bank set up in UC

Nov Remodeling of Gist Hall and expansion of marine laboratory in Trinidad • SLC excludes at-large representatives

Fall HSU applies to sell beer and wine on campus • enrollment drops from 1975-76 high of 7,706 to 7,611

1977

Jan HSU Social-Emotional Climate Committee formed in dormitories

Feb Disabled Students program initiated • Humboldt County experiences serious drought and water shortage • controversy over expansion of Redwood National Park

Mar Wrestlers, under coach Frank Cheek, win second in NCAA division III tournament

Apr Serious enrollment decline, especially in social sciences and humanities

May Professor Bobby Lake is "messenger to mankind" for flying saucer people

Jun Charles Fulkerson, Roscoe Peithman retire

Oct Student member added to CSUC trustees

Nov Mandatory credit/no credit system in all activity courses

Fall Wooden windows replaced with metal in Founders Hall • AIR Center opens to improve academic advising • expansion of library completed • Cooperative Education begun through Career Development Center

1978

Feb Campus Center for Appropriate Technology housed in Buck House • HSU and Arcata agree to cease HSU's physical growth to the north, west, and south

Mar Campus open house for community • administration building named Siemens Hall • basketball team in division III playoffs

Apr Plus/minus grading system replaces trial decimal system • shortage of funds for intercollegiate athletic programs

May Softball coach Lynn Warner named Coach of the Year for Golden State Conference • ed/psych building renamed Harry Griffith Hall • baseball field is site for new science building

Sep Oceanography research vessel *Catalyst* sinks on way to Crescent City

Oct Legislature authorizes collective bargaining in CSUC • enrollment declines to 6,735

1979

Jan Arsonist sets fire to forestry building; classes relocated by Monday morning

Feb Frank Cheek's wrestlers win FWC championship • men's basketball, under coach Jim Cosentino, ties for first in FWC, first time since 1956

Spr First issue of *Forum,* a campus journal

May Marine lab renamed Telonicher Marine Lab

Sum Humboldt Village II (37 trailers) closed

Oct State mandates Graduate Writing Proficiency Examination • 7,582 enrolled • Arcata Drive-in Movie closes • The Great Humboldt Spirit Celebration rejuvenates campus and community participation in homecoming; alumni king and queen chosen from class of '17

1980

Jan Oceanography gets research vessel, *Malaguena*

Feb Mud slide causes evacuation of Cypress Hall; repairs not completed until Oct

Mar Kathryn Corbett retires • intercollegiate baseball dropped

Apr Joni Ferris All-Indian Men's and Women's Basketball Tournament held in HSU gyms

May College Cove popular for "natural" sunbathing

Oct Forestry building reopened after 19-month closure • CFA and UPC compete to be faculty and staff representative in collective bargaining • Students for Peace organized • Phoenix Club rises out of the ashes

Nov Engineering building renamed Van Matre Hall • child development building named for Ralph Swetman • UC lounge named Karshner Lounge • Nelson Hall meeting room named Goodwin Forum • CSUC initiates plan for post-tenure review of faculty • men's cross-country, under Jim Hunt, wins regional NCAA division II title • Institute for Research and Creative Projects has Theodore Ruprecht as first director

1981

Feb   Former dean, Kate Buchanan dies; all-purpose room in University Center named for her • Frank Cheek's wrestlers win fifth straight FWC title

Mar   Flap over HSU business competition with downtown merchants

Apr   Conservation Unlimited wins Tucson Wildlife Conclave • hacky-sack fad on campus • Wilmer Bohlmann dies • Disability Awareness Day held

Fall   Football team defeats UC Davis for first time since 1969

Nov   Decline in enrollment blamed on increased fees • cheerleaders reappear, first time since 1976

1982

Jan   Business has most majors (716); forestry down to 246

Mar   Bar code system implemented for checking out library books • A national magazine lists HSU as one of 31 "lesser known but of high quality" institutions in the U.S.

Apr   Lanphere-Christensen Dunes expanded from 183 to 213 acres

Spr   Five schools renamed colleges, still have HPE and ISSP divisions • Larry Kerker, head of HPE, dies in 25th year of service • Delta Sigma Phi reactivated

May   Glenn Dumke, CSUC chancellor for 20 years, retires; replaced by Ann Reynolds • engineering and biological sciences building and geodesic greenhouse completed • retirees include William Jackson and Dave Smith • alumni association makes another effort at a yearbook (*Sempervirens* was published through 1966, *The Lamp* in 1977 and 1978)

Jun   Highest number of graduates in HSU history: 1,174 bachelor's, 144 master's

Sum   Campus hosts National Women's Studies conference

Fall   Men's Far Western Conference and women's Golden State Conference merge into Northern California Athletic Conference • third floor of Sunset Hall goes co-ed • Cypress Hall has unstable hillside • 207 fewer FTEs

Nov   Joe Trainor dies in 21st year at Humboldt • university seal features Founders Hall

Dec   Draft resisters face cuts in financial aid • Ken Chaffey retires after 32 years

1983

Jan   Budget cuts by state produce fee hikes

Feb   M.S. in environmental engineering approved • wrestlers win sixth conference title in seven years • chancellor Reynolds visits HSU for first time

Mar   First Women's History Week observed • first Peace Week • Tom Wood is NCAC coach of the year

Apr   16th annual film festival includes workshop by actress Nina Foch • forestry students win conclave at Northern Arizona U.

May   Entry level mathematics exam required of all CSU students • Lynn Warner is NCAC coach of the year for her co-champ softball team • Jefferson Starship concert in Redwood Bowl • Golden Handshake retirement offered to faculty; retirees include Milt Dobkin, Don Strahan, Bob Kittleson

Fall   Enrollment planning and management task force promotes recruiting and retention • beginning of Business Administration night class program • computerized check-out system in library

Sep   Nude bathing banned at College Cove • Cypress Hall reopened • food service's Rathskeller renamed The Depot; Athenaeum closed • Bette Lowery heads HPE • Partnership Campaign is launched

Oct   CFA and CSU negotiate first contract

Nov   JeDon Emenhiser and Ed Del Biaggio are new vice presidents

Dec   Debate over U.S. invasion of Grenada

1984

Jan   Engineering and biological sciences building closed down by support system flaws

Feb   HSU draft resister Ben Sasway gets two-year sentence for refusing to register

Mar   Low enrollment raises talk of faculty layoffs • some faculty receive $2,500 Exceptional Meritorious and Professional Promise awards

May   "Reflections on the Future" held, with faculty brainstorming on HSU's strengths and weaknesses • Frank Wood retires • KHSU receives grant to increase its wattage and double its range

Fall   Michael Wartell becomes vice president of academic affairs

Sep   Remodeled Van Matre Hall occupied by geology and computer center • CIS major approved • enrollment declines to 6,113 students (5,709 FTE) • engineering and biological sciences building reopened after its third closure

Oct   Donna Zacarro campaigns for her mother, vice presidential candidate Geraldine Ferraro • student fees reach $684 per year

Nov   School's worst football season, 0-10 • HSU receives papers of Donald Clausen, 18-year congressman from this district

Win   Emeritus Faculty Association founded

1985

Feb   Wrestlers win NCAC again • basketball team's 21-8 is best record in Humboldt history

Mar   *Getting Out,* theatre arts production, qualifies for National American Collegiate Theatre Festival at JFK Center in Washington, D.C. • Eugene Flocchini dies • Frank Devery, who retired in 1974, dies

Apr   Chi Phi fraternity forms

May   Students protest South African apartheid • former ASB president Bill Crocker appointed student member of CSU board of trustees • Tom Wicker lectures as part of Hadley Series • NBC sportscaster Dick Enberg chairs HSU Parent Fund Drive • Don Strahan dies • Jean Stradley retires

Jun   Homer Balabanis receives honorary doctorate in Fine Arts from HSU

Fall   Academic reorganization: new colleges of behavioral and social sciences; natural resources; health, education, and professional services; business and technology; creative arts and humanities; ISSP abolished • lottery funds aid student education and sponsor special speakers • Art Stegman and Charles Yocum die • Lee Badgett becomes dean for college of business and technology • temporary athletic director Chuck Lindemenn creates assistant athletic director position to promote athletics • cost for off-campus student estimated at $5,500 per year • rape, drugs, and liquor cause concern

Oct   Linus Pauling speaks on campus

Nov   Outbreak of AIDS anticipated by health center • Accuracy in Academe to monitor "liberal" professors • Bud Van Deren resigns as football coach after 20 years

Dec   Virginia Rumble retires • Estelle McDowell dies: daughter of early benefactor William Preston and '37 grad

1986

Jan   Friendship Lab opens in Founders Hall • Bella Lewitsky dance company visits • Humboldt Symphony conductor Madeline Schatz resigns • Dave Smith retires

Feb   Aviary completed for wildlife • Mike Dolby is football coach • Helen Everett, librarian from 1939-67, dies • HSU has telecommunication capability

Mar   Touring evangelist Jed Smock performs on Quad • SLC and Lumberjack Enterprises feud over student representation

Apr   *Lumberjack* ranked among top 12 college newspapers in nation • skateboarding fad

Jun   *Lumberjack* editor suspended for making political endorsements

Sep   HSU converts back to semester system • Arcata Hotel reopens after remodeling • football squad called 'Jack Attack

Oct   Lumberjack Days moved to fall • reentry students becoming more of a factor: 40% of student body is over 25; Phoenix Club reactivates, and a Reentry Center is established in House 55 • enrollment plunges from 6,220 to 5,865 • CSU admission requirements stiffen: more English, math, and foreign language • AIDS Awareness task force established • 125 additional acres given to Lanphere-Christensen Dunes • rally on Quad protests U.S. involvement in Nicaragua • David Halberstam speaks on campus

Nov   Washington Ballet performs • Lambda Sigma Nu becomes only campus sorority

Dec   More budget cuts threaten layoffs

1987

Jan   Former journalism instructor Alann Steen kidnapped by terrorists in Beirut, Lebanon

Feb   Wells Fargo donates abandoned bank building for an HSU Museum of Natural History • conflict between AS and UC over raising student fees • Don Christensen named vice president of university relations • Richard Leakey lectures

Mar   Theatre arts hosts national event, American College Theatre Festival • efforts to form an HSU student employee union fail • HSU commission on intercollegiate athletics recommends return to NCAA division III status

Sep   Enrollment grows • Lee Bowker is new dean of behavioral and social sciences • sale of Coca Cola banned at Lumberjack Days as protest against their business with South Africa • Vern Henricks becomes assistant athletic director

Oct   Center for Community Development receives grant to teach science and math to Native Americans at Happy Camp High School • jazz musician Dizzy Gillespie performs • Jim Hunt retires • pop singer Madonna donates $700,000 of equipment to theatre arts

Nov   Todd Young Report criticizes administration • Don Lawson retires after 22 years • 385-acre tree farm given to HSU for forestry department to conduct research on hardwoods

Dec   HSU chosen to host CSU's Summer Arts

1988

Feb   McCrone delivers "State of the University" message to faculty • Janet Spinas and Tom Knight retire • condoms sold in cigarette machines • SLC proposes commencement pledge not to spoil the environment

Mar Robert Everding is dean of creative arts

Aug Smoking banned in campus buildings • Allison Weber becomes first woman chair of California State Students' Association

Oct Jessie Turner Woodcock, 1917 graduate and last living charter member of Alumni Association, dies at age 92

Nov Modern Jazz Quartet performs • cross-country wins NCAC • YES celebrates 20th anniversary

1989

Mar *Lumberjack* observes 60 years of publication • satirist Mark Russell appears on campus • Film Festival celebrates 22 years

Apr HSU's 75th anniversary • Marching Lumberjacks' 20th birthday • Gay Awareness Week

May Women's softball wins NCAC

Aug Summer Arts sculptor John Roloff creates *Humboldt Ship*

Oct *US News & World Report*: "HSU 12th best in West"

Nov Time capsule buried on site of Student & Business Services Building, to be opened in 2065

1990

Jan Frank Cheek's wrestlers win NCAC for 9th time in 13 years

Apr Ann Reynolds resigns as CSU chancellor

May Master Plan calls for maximum of 8,000 FTEs at Humboldt

Aug Acting chancellor Ellis McCune labels CSU budget "the worst the California State University system has ever seen"

Nov Student & Business Services Building completed

Dec Founders Hall vacated for remodeling • HSU has more forestry majors than UC Berkeley or University of Washington

1991

Feb Moves to "multiculturalize" curriculum

Mar Fred Whitmire, HSU Hall of Fame athlete, named new football coach

Apr Cultural Diversity Week • Barry Munitz is new CSU chancellor • women's softball wins 3rd conference crown in a row

May Approval of plan to reduce number of colleges from seven to four

Aug 11.5% of HSU students are from minority groups • Homer Balabanis dies at age 93

Sep Record enrollment: 7,824

Oct Associated Students establishes "Columbus Myth-Free Zone"

Nov Former student and faculty member Alann Steen freed after a hostage for five years in Lebanon

1992

Feb Library gets new computerized catalog system • Jesus Christ Awareness Week held

Mar Creekview Apartments completed • Cultural Diversity Week celebrated • Chancellor Munitz names HSU the Center for Resolution of Environmental Disputes

Apr Major earthquake hits Humboldt County, but campus damage is minimal • Rick Botzler of wildlife named CSU's outstanding professor

Aug Newly remodeled bookstore opens

Major Gifts

Since 1985

Scholarship Trusts

Smullin Trust — from media investor William Smullin, a $150,000 scholarship trust for undergraduates from Northern California.

Cornelius Siemens Scholarship — a $100,000 scholarship trust in memory of the university's former president, established by his wife Olga Siemens-Turner.

Latvian Student Exchange Program — $90,000 from alumnus Samuel Chapin and the Lynn R. & Karl E. Prickett Fund allows Latvian students to study art at Humboldt for periods of one year.

Abdulkadir Al-Qadi Fund — $10,000 from alumnus Abdulkadir Al-Qadi assists students from the Middle East studying at Humboldt.

Maggie Griffin Scholarship Trust — an initial $25,000 gift from Glenna and Robert Cook established this trust to assist students of Yurok descent.

Frank A. and Myrtle M. Fick Memorial Scholarship — an initial $30,000 gift from alumnus Reuel Fick in honor of his parents helps students preparing for a teaching career.

Bancroft Scholars — retired accountant Lavina Bancroft, whose late husband Dwight was a musician with Lawrence Welk and Bing Crosby, has given over $21,000 in scholarships to Humboldt business and music students.

Rumble Award for Excellence in Botany — alumni Earl and Virginia Rumble enrich the lives of graduate students going on to doctoral work or to become teachers or researchers.

Library

Corrine J. and Gus A. Nordstrom Main Room — honoring the McKinleyville couple who gave the university library its first significant trust.

Humboldt State Parent Fund — $40,000 for new collections.

Pacific Telesis and Pacific Bell — collections for the school of business administration.

Distinguished Lecture Series

Hadley Distinguished Lecture — lectures by notable journalists funded by the Gordon Hadley Memorial Academic Trust, administered by Monica Hadley.

Harry S. Kieval Lectures in Mathematics — funded by HSU's former math professor.

Monroe E. Spaght Distinguished Lecture Series — lectures by prominent business leaders funded by alumnus Monroe Spaght.

Frank Watson Memorial Symposium on Ethics and Business — established by alumnus Po Chung in honor of one of his undergraduate professors, Frank Watson.

Art & Photographic Collections

Swanlund Collection — Sam Swanlund of Eureka donated a $55,000 turn-of-the-century photographic collection (glass plates, acetate negatives).

West African and Asian Collections — 562 pieces of West African art and over 200 Asian artifacts donated by alumna Marjorie Harper Jensen and former economics instructor Bernhardt Jensen.

Contemporary Art — alumna Nona Crum donated a $17,000 painting by Alaskan Sydney Laurence.

Salvador Dali's "Crucifixion" — alumnus Denby Lark gave this etching

Classrooms & Laboratories

Watson Case Room — for the school of business administration from alumnus Po Chung.

Bank of America Case Room — donated to business administration by BankAmerica Foundation.

Student study lounges — five lounges constructed by the Humboldt State Parent Fund.

Enterprise and Information Teaching Lab — 27 stations, donated by IBM, Pacific Telesis, Pacific Bell, Intel, Simpson Timber, Simpson Paper, Louisiana-Pacific, Bank of America, Schmidbauer Lumber, Blue Lake Forest Products, Cox Cable.

Friendship Microcomputer Lab — 25 stations, donated by Apple Computer and the Humboldt State Parent Fund.

24-station lab — donated by Convergent Technologies

Macintosh Lab — 25 stations, begun with a $50,000 anonymous donation.

IBM Lab — 30 stations, 19 printers, donated by IBM.

10-station lab — donated by AT&T and Humboldt State Parent Fund.

Equipment

IBM multimedia system — donated to Native American studies.

Sun Microsystems' 410 workstation — donated to chemistry department.

NEXT computer — given for academic research.

Atomic absorption spectrophotometer —chemistry got this $16,500 gift from Pacific Gas & Electric.

Lighting control console — $15,000 gift to Van Duzer Theatre from S.H. Crowell Foundation.

Cabin cruiser — a $9,100 gift from Dr. and Mrs. John Kramer.

Two Geographical Information Systems — a gift of Sierra Pacific Industries.

Research

Schatz Solar Hydrogen Project — L.W. Schatz, founder of General Plastics, contributed $760,000 to this project converting sunlight into hydrogen gas and then, through fuel cells, into electricity.

Coors Brewing / Sea Grant Project — a $3,000 gift from Coors Brewing/Andrew Rosaia Co. sparked a $20,000 grant for a pilot marsh to capture dairy runoffs.

L.W. Schatz Demonstration Tree Farm — a 385-acre tree farm for research plus an endowment: total value estimated at $1.6 million.

Forestry research — annual $2,000 grant from Champion International facilitates faculty research and participation in professional groups.

College Forest — HSU conducts ongoing research in a 310-acre forest on loan from Pacific Lumber.

Teacher Preparation

Trust fund — alumna Alice Whitson established it to benefit the teacher preparation program.

Grant — AETNA Life & Casualty Foundation provides $2,500 to $5,000 annually for HSU's teacher preparation program to assist Native American high school students in the Hoopa-Willow Creek area.

Natural History Museum

More than $600,000 in private support helped in constructing HSU's Natural History Museum. Wells Fargo Bank donated the museum building ($435,000 value). The Katherine L. Morningstar Trust gave $150,000 for bank-to-museum conversion. Humboldt Area Foundation's $58,000 helped purchase showcases. A 2,000 piece fossil collection was bought from Hilda and Tom Maloney with $100,000 of private funds and lottery grants.

Other Gifts

J.C. Penny Internships — for undergraduates in business administration; J.C. Penny also contributes $3,000 annually in scholarships.

Pacific Gas & Electric — internship in environmental resources engineering and $2,000 "Minorities in Engineering" scholarships.

Artists-in-Schools — Mervyn's grants $7,000 annually so Humboldt County school children can travel to Van Duzer Theatre to see touring artists from the CenterArts season.

History Day — Rotary clubs and local donors give $3,000 for the history department's annual "History Day" for county schoolchildren.

Wills — more than 30 individuals have provided for the university in their wills, with one gift for $500,000.

Appendix C

HSC Improvement Association

1940-50	Arthur Gist
1940-50	J.J.Krohn (president, '40-50)
1940	George Averell
1940-43	Henry Brizard
1940-45, 47-49	S.D. Cerini
1940-50	Vernon Hunt
1940-43	Frank Tooby
1943-50	Robert Matthews
1943-45	H.L. Ricks
1944-50	Chester Connick
1945-50	Gordon Manary
1946-50	Charles Barnum

Appendix D

HSC Advisory Board

1950-73	Cornelius Siemens
1950-58	J.J. Krohn
1950-68	Donald O'Kane (chair, '50-68)
1950-55	Vernon Hunt
1950-71	Robert Matthews
1950-68	Chester Connick
1950-59	Gordon Manary
1950-53	Charles Barnum
1950-74	Edward Goodwin (chair, '68-73)
1950-56	Harold Robertson
1950-53	Henry Westbrook
1952-55	Elmer Hall
1953-57	Waldron Hyatt
1953-55	Donald Larson
1953-76	Will Patton
1954-58	Edwin Fraser
1956-74	Frank Gianoni
1956-73	William Lawson

1956-61	Kirk Cooper
1958-75	Mal Coombs
1959-71	C.J. "Happy" Hill
1959-75	Thomas McNamara
1960-63	Gilbert Oswald
1961-69, 71-76	Edward Carpenter
1961-77	Henry Troblitz
1964-65	William Kerr
1967-76	Walter Dolfini (chair, '73-77)
1969-76	Byron Miller
1969-76	Andrew Rosaia
1971-72	Michael Johnston
1971-82	Leslie Westfall
1973-87	Jack Daly, Jr (chair, '77-81)
1973-81	Gordon Hadley (chair, '81)
1974-present	Alistair McCrone
1975-83	Jeanne Johnson Nash
1975-79	Karen Russ
1976-88	William Ashley (chair, '81-83)
1976-83	Lawrence Ford
1976-present	Lawrence Lazio
1976-80	Charles Motschman, Sr
1976-80	George Schmidbauer
1976-present	Dolores Vellutini (chair, '83-85)
1977-85	Eugene Lucas
1979-89	Roger Low
1980-92	Sally Arnot (chair, '89-91)
1980-88	Ellen Dusick
1980-88	Frank Peterson
1981-89	Craig Perrone (chair, '85-89)
1982-84	Craig Hadley
1984-88	Richard Hunt
1984-present	Russel Pardoe
1984-89	Henry Sandstrom
1985-89	Marilyn Bartlett
1985-89	William Daly
1988-present	Pattison Christensen (chair '91-92)
1988-present	Gerald Cochran
1988-92	Robert Thomas
1989-present	Marilee Hadley
1989-present	Howard Hunt
1989-present	James Timmons
1989-present	David Somerville (chair, '92-)
1990-present	Beth Schafer
1991-present	Scott Holmes
1992-present	David Kaney

Appendix E

Academic Senate Chair

1961	Fred Telonicher (pro tem)
1961	Roscoe Peithman (pro tem)
1961-62	Milton Dobkin
1962-63	Ralph Roske
1963-64	Robert Dickerson
1964-65	Edward Steele
1965-66	Bob Kittleson
1966-68	Richard Ridenhour
1968-69	Don Strahan
1969-70	Alba Gillespie
1970-71	Fred Cranston
1971-72	Andrew Karoly
1972-73	Lynn Jackson
1973-74	Charles Parke
1974-75	David Craigie
1975-76	Richard Meyer
1976-77	Richard Thompson
1977-78	Charles Myers
1978-80	Jack Yarnall
1980-83	Simon Green
1983-85	Ken Lang
1985-86	Bill Daniel
1986-87	Sharon Chadwick
1987-88	Lloyd Fulton
1988-90	Marshelle Thobaben
1990-92	Jack Stoob
1992-93	Michael Goodman

Appendix F

Faculty Officers

1961-62	Fred Telonicher (Pres)
1962-63	Homer Balabanis (Pres)
1963-64	Ralph Roske (Pres)
1964-65	Milton Dobkin (Pres)
1965-66	Robert Dickerson (Pres)
1966-67	Bob Kittleson (Pres)
1967-68	Louise Watson (Pres)
1968-69	William Jackson (Pres)
1969-70	Kathryn Corbett (Pres)
1970-71	George Allen (Pres)
1971-72	Glenda Richter (Pres)
1972-73	James Householder (Pres)
1973-74	James Carroll (Pres)
	Stephen Littlejohn (Sec)
	David Craigie (Treas)
1974-75	Janice Erskine (Pres)
	Evelyn Deike (Sec)
	Terry Roelofs (Treas)
1975-76	John Pauley (Pres)
	Pat Wenger (Sec)
	Charles Snygg (Treas)
1976-77	Richard Meyer (Pres)
	Stephen Littlejohn (Sec)
	Erich Schimps (Treas)
1977-78	Robert Dickerson (Pres)
	George Maglady (Sec)
	Eleanor Ferguson (Treas)
1978-79	John Gimbel (Pres)
	William Bivens (Sec)
	David Boxer (Treas)
1979-80	Herschel Mack (Pres)
	Lloyd Fulton (Sec)
	James Gaasch (Treas)
1980-81	Roy Ryden (Pres)
	Nancy Lamp (Sec)
	William Wood (Treas)
1981-82	Janet Spinas (Pres)
	Karen Foss (Sec)
	Sheila Ross (Treas)
1982-83	Hal Jackson (Pres)
	Thea Martin (Sec)
	Kathleen Preston (Treas)

1983-84	Jack Yarnall (Pres)
	Bill Daniel (Sec)
	James Gaasch (Treas)
1984-85	John Hennessy (Pres)
	Jane Abernethy (Sec)
	David Campbell (Treas)
1985-86	Sherilyn Bennion (Pres)
	Karen Carlton (Sec)
	Merle Friel (Treas)
1986-87	Bill Tanner (Pres)
	Marshelle Thobaben (Sec)
	Lewis Bright (Treas)
1987-88	Linda Anderson (Pres)
	Aimee Langlois (Sec)
	Merle Friel (Treas)
1988-89	Linda Anderson (Pres)
	Maryanne Levine (Sec)
	Ben Allen (Treas)
1989-90	Ben Allen (Pres)
	Maryanne Levine (Sec)
	Merle Friel (Treas)
1990-91	Ben Allen (Pres)
	Susan MacConnie (Sec)
	Linda Sievers (Treas)
1991-92	Wendy Woodward (Pres)
	Linda Sievers (Sec)
	Sam Sonntag (Treas)
1992-93	James GAasch (Pres)
	Simon Green (Sec)
	Ann Burroughs (Treas)

Appendix G

Scholar of the Year

1986	Yung Park (political science)
1987	Kenneth Aalto (geology)
1988	Ralph Gutierrez (wildlife)
1989	Robert Gearhart (engineering)
1990	Samuel Oliner (sociology)
	Pearl Oliner (education)
1991	Marshelle Thobaben (nursing)
1992	Karen Foss (speech)
1993	Roland Lambertson (math)

Appendix H

Outstanding Professor

1964-65	Harry Griffith (education)
	Fred Telonicher (zoology)
1965-66	John Gimbel (history)
1966-67	Reese Bullen (art)
1967-68	John Gimbel (history)
1968-69	Melvin Schuler (art)
1969-70	Theodore Ruprecht (economics)
1970-71	John Pauley (theatre)
1971-72	Frederick Cranston (physics)
1972-73	John DeMartini (biology)
1973-74	Donald Mahler (education)
1974-75	William Thonson (art)
1975-76	Henry Tropp (math)
1976-77	Yung Park (political science)
1977-78	William Jackson (business)
1978-79	James Smith, Jr. (botany)
1979-80	Donald Hauxwell (wildlife)
1980-81	David LaPlantz (art)
1981-82	Thomas Clark (chemistry)
1982-83	Gary Brusca (biology)
1983-84	John Longshore (geology)
1984-85	James Welsh (biology)
1985-86	Jerneral Cranston (theatre)
1986-87	John Morgan (psychology)
1987-88	(no nominee)
1988-89	Timothy Lawlor (biology)
1989-90	Phyllis Chinn (math)
1990-91	Ronald Fritzsche (fisheries)
1991-92	Richard Botzler (wildlife)
1992-93	Karen Carlton (English)

Appendix I

Alumni Who's Who

1960	George Hogan ('33)
1961	Kenneth Cooperrider ('29)
1962	Jessie Turner Woodcock ('17)
1963	Monroe Spaght ('26)
1964	James Hemphill ('35)
1965	Charles Fulkerson ('39)
1966	Oden Hansen ('38)
1967	Walter Dolfini ('31)
1968	Virgil Hollis ('38)
1969	Paul Ely ('34)
1970	Ruth Carroll ('34)
1971	Everett Watkins ('39)
1972	Sima Jarvinen Baker ('21)
1973	Doug Peterson ('59)
1974	Eldridge Hunt ('49)
1975	Dorothy King Young ('23)
1976	Estelle McDowell ('26)
1977	William Daly ('38)
1978	Gladys Smith Strope ('44)
1979	Delphine Belotti ('27)
1980	Michael Fielding ('57)
1981	Lanette Rousseau ('39)
1982	William Hale ('27)
1983	Ugo Giuntini ('34)
1984	Howard Goodwin ('42)
	Harvey Harper ('38)
1985	Stanley Roscoe ('43)
1986	James Joseph ('58)
1987	Grant Ferguson ('43)
1988	Henry Trione ('40)
	Albert Frakes ('62)
1989	Stanley Colwell ('40)
	Rod Belcher ('42)
	Floyd Bettiga ('54)
	Paul Corbin ('67)
1990	Frederic Hibler ('40)
	Scott Holmes ('60)
1991	Richard Ridenhour ('54)
	Robert Eggers ('55)
1992	Holly Hosterman ('77)
	Paul Lubitz ('77)

Alumni Association Presidents

1924-25	Hugh Stewart
1926	Edna Stevens
1927	Ruth Cartwright Spinas
1928	Ruth Stewart
1929-30	Carl McDonald
1931	Lena Moll Gillmore
1932	Mildred Moe Sears
1933	Alta McElwain Monroe
1934	James Spiering
1935	George Monroe
1936	Clyde Patenaude
1937	Ethel Pedrassini Scott
1938	Denise Wills
1939	Les Stromberg
1940	Walter Schocker
1941-42	William Morehouse
1943	Hally Jones Irwing
1944	Arthur Bryant
1945	Lewis Ehrlich
1946	Edward Goodwin
1947	Carl Owen
1948	James Cady
1949	Forrest Waters
1950	Mildred Moe Sears
1951-52	Everett Watkins
1953	Estelle Preston McDowell
1954	Sylvia Jacobsen Carlson
1955	Earl Rumble
1956	Margaret More Telonicher
1957	Earl Biehn
1958	James Palmer
1959	Richard Blackburn
1960	Francis Stebbins
1961-62	Jon Mitts
1963	Larry Mitchell
1964-65	Richard Ridenhour
1966-67	Lanette Rousseau
1968	Asta Cullberg
1969	Francis Moore
1970-72	Emmalena Thomson
1973-74	Ruth Carroll
1975-76	George Eue
1977	Ruth Carroll
1978	Elinor Jamieson
1979-81	Grant Ferguson
1982-83	Margorie Rodgers
1984-85	Karen Bentley
1986-87	Joe Castillo
1988	Arnie Braafladt
1989-91	Cindy Stockly
1992-93	Gwynna Morris

Homecoming Royalty

1946-47	Frances Brizard
1947-48	Mary Dolf
1948-49	Zala Bralich
1949-50	Barbara Hackett
1950-51	Helen Gross
1951-52	Shirley Pitlock
1952-53	Donna Martzall
1953-54	Jacki Ambrozini
1954-55	Donna Mae Douglas
1955-56	Fern Fowler
1956-57	Tonya Rocha
1957-58	Kris Church
1958-59	Lynn Cannam
1959-60	Donna Cleveland
1960-61	Rose Holmquist
1961-62	Linda Arvola
1962-63	Lynn Loebner
1963-64	Ann Pirtle
1964-65	Sue Dresser
1965-66	Louise St. Jean
1966-67	Alice Treutlein
1967-68	Sheryl Carlson
1968-69	Mary Ann McRae
1969-70	Marilyn Moore

1970-71	Mary Kay Tyson
1971-72	Cydney Clayton
1979	Jessie Turner Woodcock
	Harry Wandling
1980	Marjorie Jensen
	Homer Spellenberg
1981	Elta Cartwright
	Joseph Branstetter
1982	Leo Sullivan
	Dee Sullivan
1983	Archie Forson
	Estelle McDowell
1984	Zdenka McGaraghan
	Harold Brogan
1985	Jim Hemphill
	Kathryn Stewart
1986	Dorothy Gulliksen
	Leland Cloney
1987	Everett Watkins
	Kathryn Murray
1988	Collis Mahan
	Jennie Banducci
1989	Alex & Nathalie Smith
1990	Carl Owen
	Marian Howatt
1991	Josephine Tyson
	Curtis Wilson
1992	Marianne Lambert Pinches
	Milton Carlson

Student Body Presidents

1914	Leslie Graham
1922	Allen Otto
1923	Hartsel Gray
1924	Howard Trueblood
1925-26	Walter Jack
1926 (F)	Alfred Ames
1927 (S)	Monroe Spaght
1927 (F)	Shirley Cameron Mace
1928 (S)	Glenn Rusk
1928-29	Allan McCurdy
1929-30	Percy Homer Spellenberg
1930-31	Glenn Waldner
1931-32	George Gregory
1932-33	Wayne Simpson
1933-34	James Hemphill
1934-35	Charles Timmons
1935-36	Eleanor Renfro Jones
1936-37	Oden Hansen
1937-38	Robert Madsen
1938-39	Nick Barbieri
1939-40	Sherman Washburn
1940-41	Milton Earnest "Bud" Villa
1941 (F)	Forrest Waters
1941 (F)	Tom Hansen
1942 (S)	Fred Slack
1942 (F)	Clarke Nellist
1943 (S)	Jack Piersall
1943-44	Ralph E. Bryant
1944-45	Katherine Swap
1945 (F)	Marshall Rousseau
1946 (S)	John Sivert
1946-47	Leonard Conry
1947-48	Darrell Brown
1948 (F)	Mark Melendy
1949 (S)	Henry Frank
1949-50	Wilbur Jensen
1950-51	Merwyn Rickey
1951-52	Francis Stebbins
1952-53	Richard Harmer
1953-54	Earl Rumble
1954-55	Dwain Haines
1955-56	Lawrence Flammer
1956-57	Michael Fielding
1957-58	Dale Callihan
1958-59	Don Peterson
1959-60	Arthur Dalianes
1960-61	Dennis Cahill
1961-62	Bill Turner
1962-63	Jack Moore
1963-64	Jack Turner
1964-65	Charles Freitas
1965-67	Robert Henry
1967 (S)	John Wooley
1967-68	Thomas Osgood
1968-69	Harold Hartman
1969-70	Waine Benedict
1970-71	Bill Richardson
1971-72	Arnold Braafladt
1972-73	Ashford Wood
1973-74	Becky Aus
1974-75	Richard Ramirez
1975-76	David Kalb
1976-77	Dan Falk
1977-78	Greg Cottrel
1978-79	Eddie Scher
1979-80	Tom Bergman
1980-81	Alison Anderson
1981-82	Jeff Lincoln
1982-83	Ross Glen
1983-84	Otis Johnson
1984-85	Bill Crocker
1985-86	Mark Murray
1986-87	Teri Carbaugh
1987-88	Al Elpusan
1988-89	Vicki Allen
1989-91	Randy Villa
1991-92	Steve Harmon
1992-93	Emma Young

Lumberjack Editors

1924-25	Lee Baird (*The Foghorn*)
1929-30	Lawrence Morris (*HSTC Rooter*)
1930-31	Joseph Stringfellow
1931-32	Buster DeMotte
1932-33	Ruth Carroll
1933-34	Gordon Hadley, Ruth Carroll
1934-35	John Bauriedel, Grace Schell
1935-36	(not published)
1936-37	Wesley Wooden, Jayn Harville
1937-38	Hope Dondero
1938-39	Jack Ellis
1939-40	Frances Nye
1940-41	Muriel Yale, Helen Hartsook
1941-42	Helen Hartsook, Sheldon Reaume
1942-43	Barbara Conoly
1943-44	Marjorie Kemper, Leigh Manley, Marjorie Briggs
1944-45	LaVerle Morley
1945-46	Donald Ray, Kathie Nuckols
1946-47	Charles Peterson
1947-48	Paul Gelfman, Vernon Whalen
1948-49	Vernon Whalen, Janet Oppenheimer
1949-50	Alfred Braun, Charlotte Marks
1950-51	Charlotte Marks, Carl Jensen, Jean Nichols
1951-52	Jean Nichols, Danforth White
1952-53	Danforth White, Dale Farris
1953-54	John Norton
1954-55	Craig Stark
1955-56	George Golding, Frances Stark
1956-57	Keith Barnhill
1957-58	Jewell Hyman; (issue ed.) Diane Anderson, Carol Kirkby, Don Neilsen, Stanley McDaniel, Martha Smith, Tony Vasquez, Bill Wallace
1958-59	Diane Anderson
1959-60	(issue ed.) Keith Barnhill, Don Carlton, Carolyn Caulley, Donna Cleveland, Mary Ann Miner, Betsy Joyce, Barbara Oberdorf, Judy Ross, Lu Vlaardinger, Vicky Williams, Cliff

	Hawthorne, Bill Guimond, Will Dublin, Hugh Clark
1960-61	Hugh Clark
1961-62	Cliff Hawthorne, Duane Oneto
1962-63	Duane Oneto, Dale G. Potts
1963-64	Martha Gabriel, Chuck Freitas
1964-65	Dale Potts, William Huffman, Jr
1965-66	Ken Bryant, Al Brewer
1966-67	Al Brewer, Don Rubin
1967-68	Dave Miers, Jim Linn, Abby Abinati
1968-69	Ron Harding, Al Steen, Tom Sheets
1969-70	Tom Sheets, Mike Stockstill, Lois Esser
1970-71	Lois Esser, Mike Stockstill, Richard Larson
1971-72	Hatton Kashdan, Valerie Ohanian
1972-73	Valerie Ohanian, Paul Brisso
1973-74	Brian Alexander, Linda Fjeldsted
1974-75	Linda Fjeldsted, Robin Piard
1975-76	Keith Till, Sally Connell
1976-77	Sally Connell, Katie Shanley
1977-78	Lindsey McWilliams, Andrew Alm
1978-79	Andrew Alm, Brian S. Akre
1979-80	Katie Muldoon, Danae Seemann
1980-81	Danae Seeman, Laura Dominick
1981-82	Tad Weber, Chris Crescibene
1982-83	Chris Crescibene, Jennifer McGauley
1983-84	Pat Stupek, Adam Truitt
1984-85	Adam Truitt, Robert Couse-Baker,
Joyce	Mancini, Cesar Soto
1985-86	Chris Roeckl, Rod Boyce, Tom Verdin
1986-87	Tom Verdin, Mark Anderson, Steve Salmi
1987-88	David Montesino, David Kirkman, Phyllis Quackenbush
1988-89	Kim Lococo, Vedder McCaustland
1989-90	Paul Elias, Andrew Silva
1990-91	Kie Relyea, T.S. Heie
1991-92	Colleen Futch, Leslie Weiss, P.J. Johnston
1992-93	Jim Waters

Appendix N

Athletics Hall of Fame

1955	Earl Meneweather	Ftbl
1956	Dr. Billy Lee	Bsktbl, Ftbl, Tns
1957	Dobe Harrison	Bsbl, Ftbl
1958	Leonard Longholm	Ftbl, Bsktbl, Trk
1959	Elta Cartwright	Trk
1960	Francis Moore	Ftbl, Bsktbl
1961	Cliff Branstetter	Ftbl, Bsbl, Bsktbl, Tns, Bxng, Glf
1962	Darrell Brown	Bsktbl, Bsbl, Trk
1963	Frank Saunderson	Ftbl, Bsktbl, Tns
1964	Edwin Oliveira	Bsktbl, Ftbl, Bsbl
1965	Lee Seidell	Bsktbl
1966	Ray Mechals	Ftbl, Bsktbl, Bsbl
1967	Claude Eshleman	Bsktbl, Trk
1968	Francis Givins	Ftbl, Bsktbl, Trk
1969	James McAuley	Ftbl
1970	James Thompson	Ftbl, Trk
1971	Henry Cooper	Ftbl
1972	Leo Sullivan	Ftbl, Bsktbl
1973	Robert Dunaway	Ftbl, Bsktbl
1974	Fred Whitmire	Ftbl
1975	Vester Flanagan	Ftbl, Trk
1976	Ken Dunaway	Ftbl, Bsktbl, Bsbl
1977	Delores Sullivan Henders	Trk
	George Ibarretta	Bsbl
	Drew Roberts	Ftbl, Bsktbl, Bsbl
1978	John Burman	Ftbl
	Gordon Schroeder	Ftbl, Trk
	Katie Walsh	Sftbl
1979	Earl Barnum	Ftbl, Trk
	Gary Tuttle	Trk
	Lynn Warner	Bdmtn, Trk, Vllybl, FldHky, Bsktbl, Sftbl
1980	Warren Baker	Ftbl, Bsktbl, Bsbl, Trk
	Michelle Nance	Trk
	Cecil Stephens	Ftbl
1981	Bill Hook	Ftbl, Trk
	Bob Lawson	Bsbl, Bsktbl
	Phil Sarboe	Coach
	Pat Susan	Bsktbl, Sftbl, Trk, Vllybl, Bdmtn

1982	Len Gotshalk	Ftbl
	Fred Iten	Ftbl, Bsktbl, Trk, Bxng
	Barbara Smith	FldHky, Bsktbl, Sftbl
	Fred Telonicher	Coach
1983	Janet Ferguson	Trk
	Bill Scobey	Trk, X-cntry
	Sal Sino	Ftbl
1984	Paul Huff	Ftbl, Trk
	Karen Muene	Swmng
	Doug Stone	Wrsln
1985	Tony Keith	Ftbl
	Donna Renaud	Swmng
	Felix Rogers	Bsktbl
1986	Jeff Fern	Wrsln
	George Psaros	Ftbl
	Sue Rodearmel	Swmng
1987	Sue Grigsby	Trk
	Joe Myers	Bsktbl
	Glenn Wallace	Ftbl, Bsktbl
1988	Michelle Betham	Trk
	Alison Child	Vllybl
	Chuck Giannini	Ftbl
	Kris Henry	Wrsln
1989	Grace Brosnahan	Swmng
	Jane Eilers	Vllybl
	Ed White	Ftbl
	Eric Woolsey	Wrsln
1990	Cheryl Clark	Sftbl
	Chuck Huntington	Sccr
	Ced Kinser	Coach, trainer
	Chris Rosvold	Bsktbl
	Chuck Smead	Trk
1991	Kathy Dolan	X-cntry, Trk
	Debbie Hungerford	Sftbl, Vllybl
	Frank Logan	Swmng
	Marty Nellis	Wrsln
1992	Steve Alexander	Bsktbl
	Deanna Allen	Sftbl, Vllybl
	Barbara Culbertson	Vllybl, Sftbl
	Danny Grimes	X-cntry, Trk
	R.W. Hicks	Ftbl
	Sharon Powers	Trk, X-cntry
	Manuel Simas	Ftbl

Coaching Records

Archery — Co-ed

| 1967-72 | Evelyn Deike | (no records) |

Badminton — Women's

| 1960-78 | Leela Zion | (no records) |

Baseball — Men's

	Coach	Won	Lost	Tied
1923	Altho Sly	6	0	0
1924-25	Bert Smith	5	5	0
1926-27	Cy Falkenberg	4	12	1
1928-37	Fred Telonicher	33	11	3
1937	Telonicher/Moore	2	1	0
1938	Telonicher/Hemphill	2	2	0
1939	Walt Oglesby	2	2	0
1940-41	Harry Griffith	1	0	0
1947	Larry Pape	8	4	0
1948	Warren Conrad	4	6	0
1949	Louis Tsoutsouvas	3	6	1
1950	Ted Staffler	4	8	0
1951-53	Phil Sarboe	26	18	12
1954-68	Ced Kinzer	235	146	6

Basketball — Men's

	Coach	Won	Lost
1923-25	Bert Smith	6	3
1925-27	Fred Falkenberg	2	7
1927-38	Fred Telonicher	12	26
1938-39	Herb Hart	5	3
1939-42	Harry Griffith	28	23
1942-45	Marty Mathiesen	4	16

1946-47	Joseph Forbes	9	11
1947-48	Warren Conrad	4	8
1948-49	Joseph Forbes	8	10
1949-51	Jack Whetstone	2	26
1951-52	Paul Sarboe	4	13
1952-53	Joseph Forbes	11	10
1953-64	Francis Givins	100	140
1964-65	Henry Cooper	6	13
1965-75	Dick Niclai	70	177
1975-76	Kim Kellenberg	3	21
1976-81	Jim Cosentino	79	56
1981-	Tom Wood	166	171

Basketball — Women's

	Coach	Won	Lost
1973-76	Lynn Warner	6	27
1976-78	Diann Laing	16	18
1978-79	Marcia Walker	4	1
1979-80	Mary Hosley	6	11
1980-82	Diann Laing	8	29
1983-85	Cinda Rankin	18	58
1985-87	Chris Conway	13	39
1987-	Pam Martin	72	81

Boxing — Men's

| 1947-49 | Grady Lawrence | 1st vs high schools, 4th intercollegiate |

Cross-Country — Men's

FWC / NCAC		Best finish
1959	Robert Doornik	3rd
1961-62	Ford Hess	5th
1963	Robert Doornik	5th
1964-66	Ford Hess	3rd
1967-86	Jim Hunt	1st ('74, '77, '79-'81)
1987-	David Wells	1st ('88, '90-'92)

Cross-Country — Women's

NCAC		Best finish
1977	Joli Sandoz	(no records)
1978	Jackie Yapp	4th
1979	Lloyd Wilson	4th
1980-	David Wells	2nd

Field Hockey — Women's

1960-68	Leela Zion	(no records)
1969-78	Lynn Warner	(no records)

Football — Men's

	Coach	Won	Lost	Tied
1924	Bert Smith	1	0	0
1925	Cy Falkenberg	1	3	0
1927-34	Fred Telonicher	8	23	2
1935-37	Charley Erb	15	6	1
1938-40	Herb Hart	12	8	0
1941	Earl Hoos	2	5	1
1946-47	Joseph Forbes	10	7	1
1948	Louis Tsoutsouvas	6	3	0
1949-50	Ted Staffler	0	12	2
1951-65	Phil Sarboe	104	37	5
1966-85	Bud Van Deren	97	101	4
1986-90	Mike Dolby	17	34	2
1990-	Fred Whitmire	13	9	0

Golf — Men's

	Coach	Won	Lost
1947	Larry Pape	0	1
1948-49	Harold Bishop	1	1
1950-51	Lloyd Whetstone	2	1
1952	Elwood Studivant	1	3
1953, 55	Phil Sarboe	2	3
1956	Francis Givins	3	5
1957-60	Phil Sarboe	8	12
1961-63	Ford Hess	5	16
1964-69	Francis Givins	16	17

Soccer — Men's

	Coach	Won	Lost	Tied
1971	Mike Szarek	1	3	2
1972-78	Bob Kelly	37	44	12
1980-84	Chris Hopper	29	43	10
1985-	Alex Exley	82	71	11

Softball — Women's

	Coach	Won	Lost
1973-74	Barb van Putten	6	8
1975-76	Bes Chandler	5	11
1977	Barb van Putten	6	14
1978-83	Lynn Warner	66	59
1989-	Frank Cheek	162	62

Swimming — Men's

	Coach	Won	Lost
1961-62	Ralph Hassman	0	5
1963	Henry Cooper	1	3
1964-65	Phil Sarboe	1	4
1966-70	James Malone	18	19
1971-75	Larry Angelel	best finish 3rd in FWC	

Swimming — Women's

1960-66	Leela Zion	(no records)
1967	Betty Partain	(no records)

FWC / NCAC		*Best finish*
1970-79	Betty Partain	4th
1980-89	Pam Armold	5th
1989-91	Sue Rodearmel	3rd

Tennis — Men's

	Coach	Won	Lost	Tied
1933-34	Monica Wright	(no records)		
1935	Carl Owen	5	0	0
1936-39	Laverne Elmore	2	14	0
1940-47	Ellis Williamson	8	11	0
	(no team 1943-45)			
1948-49	Hermie Kroeger	3	0	0
1952	Elwood Studivant	6	0	0
1953	Francis Givins	3	3	1
1954	Birger Johnson	4	0	0
1955	Francis Givins	4	1	0
1956	Hank Yamagata	3	4	0
1957-69	Larry Kerker	47	60	0

Tennis — Women's

1984-88	Fred Siler	best finish 3rd in NCAC

Track — Men's

Versus high schools

1932-37	Fred Telonicher	7	2
1939-42	Herb Hart	3	1

FWC / NCAC		*Best finish*
1947	Joseph Forbes	3rd
1948	Birger Johnson	4th
1949	Jack Norton	4th
1952-53	Birger Johnson	4th
1954	Francis Givins	4th
1955-57	Robert Doornik	5th
1958	Gordon Schroeder	4th
1959-62	Robert Doornik	1st ('59)
1963	Bud Van Deren	6th
1964	Robert Doornik	5th
1965	Ralph Hassman	6th
1966	Robert Houston	6th
1967-85	Jim Hunt	3rd
1986-89	David Wells	3rd
1990-	James Williams	3rd

Track — Women's

1960-64	Louise Watson	(no records)
1969-75	Lynn Warner	(no records)
1976	Jim Peters	(no records)

NCAC		*Best finish*
1977-78	Joli Sandoz	5th
1979	Jackie Yapp	(no records)
1980	Lloyd Wilson	5th
1981-89	David Wells	3rd
1990-	James Williams	4th

Volleyball — Women's

	Coach	Won	Lost
1963-72	Barb van Putten	(no records)	
1973	Barb van Putten	7	1
1974-75	Bes Chandler	9	10
1976-82	Barb van Putten	50	55
1983	Lynn Warner	6	15
1984	Lori Schaffer	6	10
1985-88	Janis Rowe-Grondalski	53	64
1989	Dan Collen	19	13
1990-91	Collen/Julie Ortman	64	31

Water Polo — Men's

1966-70	James Malone	32	35
1971-79	Larry Angelel	2nd three times	

Wrestling — Men's

	Coach	Won	Lost	Tied
1959-60	Gordon Schroeder	3	3	0
1960-62	Ralph Hassman	6	11	1
1962-64	Bud Van Deren	7	17	0
1964-67	Ralph Hassman	21	14	0
1967-69	Bob Kelly	23	10	2
1969-81	Frank Cheek	182	40	4
1981-82	Eric Woolsey	5	11	0
1983-91	Frank Cheek	77	67	5

Bibliography

Almer, Torun. *A University Student Survey of Sexual Information, Attitudes and Concerns.* Unpublished M.A. thesis, Humboldt State University, June, 1975. HSU Library / Archives.

Anderson, Cindy G. *Sex Differences in Student Drug Usage at Humboldt State University.* Unpublished M.A. thesis, Humboldt State University, June, 1976. HSU Library / Archives.

Anker, Jim L. *The Establishment of Humboldt State Normal School.* Barnum Prize, unpublished, Humboldt State University, 1975. HSU Library / Archives.

Annual Ring. Vols. 1-26 (1959-1984). Humboldt State College Forestry Club. HSU Library / Archives.

Appendix to the Journal of the Senate and Assembly. 39th Session, Vol I. Sacramento: Superintendent of State Printing, 1912.

"Arcata Community Survey," Humboldt State College, 1947. HSU Library / Archives.

Balabanis, Homer P. "Knowledge . . . To What End?" An address delivered at the commencement exercises of Humboldt State College, May 29, 1964. HSU Library / Archives.

Balabanis, Homer P. *Humboldt State: The Reminiscences of Homer P. Balabanis.* Humboldt State University, 1984.

Bennett, Dick. *A History of Humboldt State College.* Barnum Prize, unpublished, Humboldt State University, 1967. HSU Library / Archives.

Brisso, Paul A. *A History of the Humboldt State University Residence Halls: Facilities and Philosophy.* Barnum Prize, unpublished, Humboldt State University, 1975. HSU Library / Archives.

Cabrillo. May, 1927.

Cadenhead, Howard M. *The History and Development of Intercollegiate Football at Humboldt State College, 1927-1965.* Unpublished M.A. thesis, Humboldt State University, August, 1969. HSU Library / Archives.

Cappel, Lawrence William. *The History of Intercollegiate Track and Field at Humboldt State College from 1930 to 1970.* Unpublished M.A. thesis, Humboldt State University, June, 1971. HSU Library / Archives.

Carranco, Lynwood, ed. *The Redwood Country.* Dubuque, IA: Kendal/Hunt Publishing Company, 1971.

Community Development. Vols. I-II (December 1966 - May, 1969). Center for Community Development, Humboldt State College. HSU Library / Archives.

Conservation Unlimited: Conservation Unlimited Poop Sheet. Humboldt State College, 1950-1969. HSU Library / Archives.

Coons, Arthur G., et al. *A Master Plan for Higher Education in California, 1960-1975.* Sacramento: California State Department of Education, 1960.

Corcoran, Michael. "Twenty Years in the Presidency." *Arcata Union*, April 9, 1970.

Coy, Owen C. *The Humboldt Bay Region, 1850-1875.* Humboldt Historical Society.

Cremin, Lawrence A. *The Transformation of the School: Progressivism in American Education, 1876-1957.* New York: A.A. Knopf, 1961.

Davies, Sarah M. *A History of Humboldt State College.* Unpublished M.A. thesis, Stanford UIniversity, 1947. HSU Library / Archives.

Dillon, Richard H. "Exploring Inner Space." Speech at dedication of HSC Library, April 7, 1963. HSU Library / Archives.

Ferguson, Janet Sue. *The Development of the Women's Athletic Program at Humboldt State University, 1925-1975.* Unpublished M.A. thesis, Humboldt State University, 1975. HSU Library / Archives.

First Biennial Report of the State Board of Education, State of California. Board of Education, 1913-1914. California State Printing Office, 1915.

Foghorn. Humboldt State Teacher's College (October 1, 1924 - May 9, 1925). HSU Library / Archives.

Forbes, Joseph M. An *Intercollegiate Athletic History of Humboldt State College, 1914-1952.* Unpublished manuscript, 1953. HSU Library / Archives.

Forbes, Joseph M. *History of Athletics: Humboldt State College, 1914-1968: The Lumberjack Story.* Unpublished manuscript, 1968. HSU Library / Archives.

Forum. Vols. 1-2 (1961-1962). HSU Library / Archives.

Forum: A Faculty and Staff Journal for Humboldt State University. Vols. 1-5 (1979-1982). HSU Library / Archives.

Gallagher, Thomas J. *HSU Landscape Master Plan.* April, 1982. HSU Library / Archives.

Graham, Patricia A. *Progressive Education" From Arcady to Academe. A History of the Progressive Education Association, 1919-1955.* Columbia University: Teachers College Press, 1967.

Graves, C. Edward. *Our Search for Wilderness.* Hicksville, New York: Exposition Press, 1975.

Harrison, Carol. "Tackling Segregation in the 60s." *Humboldt Stater,* Vol. 9, No. 2 (Spring, 1991).

Hilltopper of Humboldt State College. 1957-1968. HSU Library / Archives.

Humboldt Alumnus. 1934-1982. HSU Library / Archives.

Humboldt News Letter. Nos. 1-13 (December 29, 1943 - Christmas, 1945). HSU Library / Archives.

Humboldt State College: A Brief "Get Acquainted" Report on Some of the Major Aspects of its Program of Instruction, Services, and Campus Facilities. October, 1961. HSU Library / Archives.

Humboldt State College: Honors Colloquium. Fall, 1960. HSU Library / Archives.

Humboldt State Normal School Letter (also called *Catalogue, Bulletin, Circular of Information).* 1916- . HSU Library / Archives.

"Humboldt State University Affirmative Action Plan." February 1975. HSU Library / Archives.

Humboldt Stater. 1983-1992. HSU Library / Archives.

Jessen, Michael A. *On and Off Campus Students: A Comparison of Their Personality Characteristics and Social Attitudes.* Unpublished M.A. thesis, Humboldt State University, 1973. HSU Library / Archives.

Jones, John L. *A History of Varsity Track and Field at Humboldt State College from 1914-1965.* Unpublished M.A. thesis, Humboldt State College, 1971. HSU Library / Archives.

Karshner, Gayle B., editor. *The Way It Was.* Project of Humboldt State University's Retired Senior Volunteer Program, 1979.

Kearns, Sean. "Humboldt's Botanical Bounty." *Humboldt Stater,* Vol. 10, No. 1 (Fall, 1991).

Landsbergen, P., and L. Proctor. *Expenditure Patterns of Humboldt State Students, Faculty, and Staff.* Unpublished M.S. thesis, Humboldt State College, 1969. HSU Library / Archives.

Lewis, John H. *Wildlife Management Program.* Unpublished manuscript, 1948. HSU Library / Archives.

Marshall, Zane Omer. *A History of Industrial Arts at Humboldt State University.* Unpublished M.A. thesis, Chico State University, 1976. HSU Humboldt County Collection.

McCue, Susan E. *The History of Women's Athletics: Humboldt State University.* Barnum Prize, unpublished, Humboldt State University, 1975. HSU Library / Archives.

McDermid, Charles. *A Study of the Reading Program at College Elementary School from 1953-1957.* Unpublished M.A. thesis, Humboldt State College, 1958. HSU Library / Archives.

Mitchell-Brown, Marcus. "European Discovery and Early History of Humboldt County to the Coming of the Railroads," Humboldt Historical Society.

Mottaz, Stan. *Organizations at Humboldt State College: A Report on the History of Organizations at Humboldt State College Transmitted to the Dean of Students.* Unpublished manuscript, 1970. HSU Library / Archives.

Pacific Oceanic Olio. Nos. 1-9 (February, 1965 - November, 1969). Humboldt State College Department of Oceanography. HSU Library / Archives.

Palais, Hyman. *A Short History of Humboldt State: from Normal School to University.* Unpublished manuscript, Arcata, California, 1976. HSU Library / Archives.

Pauley, John F. *The Story of the Theatre Arts Department: Humboldt State University, 1914-1982.* Unpublished manuscript, 1984. HSU Library / Archives.

Petranek, Jan. *Humboldt State University Development Master Plan.* Unpublished manuscript, January 20, 1984. HSU Library / Archives.

Phillips, Gary O., William C. Shaw, and John D. Viale. *A Study of Expenditures by Students, Faculty and Staff of Humboldt State College, Arcata, California.* Unpublished manuscript, March 14, 1969. HSU Library / Archives.

Report on Physical Conditions of Humboldt State College, Arcata. Sacramento: State of California Department of Public Works, 1954.

Rooter (later *Lumberjack*). 1929- . Humboldt State College. HSU Library / Archives.

Ruprecht, Theodore K. *The Economic Impact of Humboldt State University on the Humboldt County Economy.* Unpublished manuscript, 1978. HSU-Humboldt County Collection.

The Salary and Staffing Crisis in the California State Colleges. Association of California State College Professors. March, 1964.

Sewall, Gilbert T. *Necessary Lessons: Decline and Renewal in American Schools.* New York: Macmillan, 1983.

Siemens, Cornelius Henry. A *Personal History.* August, 1978. HSU Library / Archives.

Spaght, Monroe E. "Concern for Character." Address, May 9, 1963. HSU Library / Archives.

Spaght, Monroe E. "What's New?" Humboldt State College commencement address, June 4, 1965. HSU Library / Archives.

Stockstill, Mike "In Memorium — Joe College." *The Lumberjack,* January 14, 1970.

Straight From Student Services. Vol. 1 (May, 1975). Humboldt State University. HSU Library / Archives.

Strayer, George D., et al. *A Report of a Survey of the Needs of California in Higher Education.* Sacramento: Department of Education and Regents of the University of California, 1948.

Survey Report on Physical Property of Humboldt State College. Sacramento: State of California Department of Public Works, 1950.

Swain, Lorna Mullen. *A Follow-Up Study of Student Withdrawals at Humboldt State College.* Unpublished M.A. thesis, Humboldt State College, May, 1954. HSU Library / Archives.

Timber: A North Coast Journal. Vol. 1, Nos. 1-2 (Spring, 1963; Spring, 1966). HSU Library / Archives.

Trepiak, Tom. *History of Athletics: Humboldt State University, 1914-1982.* Sports Information Director Publication, Arcata, California, 1982.

Trump, Marvin, and Ralph W. Jones. *Campus Master Plan for Humboldt State College.* Eureka, California, 1970.

25th Biennial Report, 1910-1912. State of California Office of the Superintendent of Public Instruction. Sacramento: State Printing Office, 1912.

Willis, Jerry. *A History of the Founding of Humboldt State College.* Barnum Prize, unpublished, Humboldt State College, 1959. HSU Library / Archives.

Wurster, Bernardi and Emmons. *Campus Master Plan: Humboldt State College.* San Francisco, California, 1965.

Yusi, Raymond D. *Humboldt State University Campus Master Plan: Revisions.* Long Beach, California, 1981.

Photo Credits

Index